# big mama's
# Old Black Pot
## recipes

A STOKE GABRIEL ENTERPRISES, INCORPORATED PUBLICATION

© 1987 by Stoke Gabriel Enterprises, Inc.
P.O. Box 12060 • Alexandria, Louisiana 71315
(318) 487-9577

Library of Congress Catalog Number 87-81836
ISBN 0-929288-00-9

*Dedicated to*
*every wife, mother and daughter*
*who toiled over a hot wood stove*
*"making-do" with whatever*
*sparse staples that were available*
*to provide for their family*
*a tasty, nourishing meal.*

*recipes*
*illustrations*
Ethel Dixon

*editors*
Charlene Johnson
Wayne Tanner

*photography*
*composition*
*printing*
Stoke Gabriel Enterprises, Inc.
Alexandria, Louisiana
(318) 487-9577
http://www.oldblackpot.com

*To all who supported and encouraged
the production of this book and to
the families of El and Ethel Dixon, we
extend a special thanks.*

Reaching back and tugging at old and almost forgotten memories — that's what *Big Mama's Old Black Pot Recipes* is all about. This cookbook is brimming with page after page of nostalgia and recipes for good old-fashioned, calorie-ladened, country-style cooking.

Meshing the old and the new makes this cookbook useful as well as entertaining. Splendid illustrations, short stories and folklore depict a way of life scarcely recorded in history books. The recipes included are simple and delicious — and have long been favorites of "country folk" as well as their kissing cousins from the city.

While pouring through old letters, photographs, journals, diaries, etc., chatting across fences with farmers and sitting on porches listening to stories about "hard times," we came to a couple of rather profound conclusions. First, the rural South has a proud heritage that must not be tucked away and forgotten. And second, "an old black pot can't be beat when you want something fit to eat."

— Editors

# HOW TO SEASON A NEW BLACK POT

A new cast iron pot must be seasoned to insure best results when cooking. The steps to follow are very simple:

(1) Wash pot thoroughly and wipe dry.

(2) Place empty pot on burner and heat until extremely hot.

(3) Carefully remove pot from burner and wipe inside of pot with cloth saturated with shortening.

(4) Place pot back on burner and heat until bottom of pot begins to smoke.

(5) Remove from heat and wipe with oil cloth thoroughly coating inside of pot. Set aside and allow to cool.

(6) After pot cools to a temperature that allows handling, wipe excess fat from pot with clean cloth.

Now you are ready to begin cooking.

# HOW TO CLEAN AN OLD BLACK POT

Extensive use of an iron pot will cause a crust to build up on the inside and outside of the pot. No amount of washing will prevent this build-up.

To clean follow this procedure:

(1) Wash pot as normal

(2) Place empty pot in an open fire, fireplace, wood heater or in campfire. Allow pot to COOK until residue is burned away.

(3) HANDLE CAREFULLY — remove from fire and set aside, allowing slow cooling until pot is cool enough to hold.

(4) Use moist sand and cloth to scrub inside and outside of pot.

Your 20 year old pot will look the same as when it was new. Wash and season pot before using.

SUPPER

# SUPPER

*"Bless the hands of those who prepared for us this food and make us thankful for these and all blessings."*

—*AMEN*

Words so softly spoken, usually before daylight and after dark, echoed from the walls of almost every country home.

Families were generally larger then than today, but everyone found a place around the table at mealtime. Food was not always in generous supply, but was filling, nourishing and well prepared.

Meat came from the smokehouse, except on Sunday; then if company came, it was fried chicken or chicken and dumplings. Vegetables were grown in the garden or even picked wild at certain times of the year. No matter, Mama was well versed in her task and accepted the responsibility of seeing that the family was present and a place prepared for each member when mealtime came around. After all, it was a time of family togetherness. Everyone sat and everyone ate . . .

—at the same time.

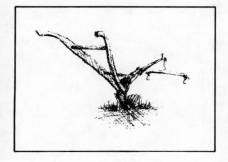

**breads**

## THE BREAD MAKER

When Papa put that window in
the kitchen — the one just to the
right of that old wood stove — he
surely must have deliberated
considerably to get it in just the
right place. Seems like the sun
was always shining through that
window.

The white cloth spread over
mounds of sourdough setting on
the window sill was a sure sign
that Mama was in the kitchen. The
warmth of the sun being absorbed
by the dough rising in that old
black tin pan sent out an aroma
that required little coaxing to have
the family to the table when the
bread came hot out of the oven.

Mama never served a meal
without bread. Whether biscuits,
loaf bread, cornbread, muffins or
plain old hot water cornbread,
there was always bread on the
table. Bread was not a luxury; it
was considered a necessity.
And the art of making bread
passed from  mother to daughter
through the generations just like
grandma's old rocker.

"We'll sure enjoy that bread
come supper and after supper
we'll enjoy the rocker."

# BIG MAMA'S SHORT'NEN BREAD

2 cups flour
2 teaspoons baking
    powder
pinch of salt
2 eggs
1/2 cup butter
1 cup sweet milk
1 teaspoon vanilla

Cream eggs and butter. Add remaining ingredients. Grease and flour a 9 inch loaf pan. Pour batter into pan.

**Bake 350 degrees — approximately 1 hour.**

*Let cool and serve with jelly or preserves.*

---

*Big Mama, Julia Pettaway, was born in 1880 in Keatchie, Louisiana, a small rural community near Shreveport. She acquired the name Big Mama, not because of stature, but because of her determined iron will to face challenges head-on and make the most of them. Married at the early age of fourteen, she was later to face the task of rearing a family of six boys and three girls alone.*

*Julia managed to acquire one hundred acres of land by sharecropping, buying and selling cattle, selling vegetables from her garden and selling butter and milk from her cows. A fruit orchard provided apples and pears. The children also picked berries that were sold on the side of the "Big Road" for ten cents a bucket. Big Mama raised her own meat, which she and the boys slaughtered, cured and smoked.*

*One of her most accomplished talents was that of making furniture — tables, chairs, desks and dressers. All were simple, but solid and lasting.*

*Julia assumed the responsibility of teaching each child to read and write. During the winter, the girls worked by her side learning to quilt, sew and cook.*

*She took great pride in her family.*

13

*breads*

# BAKING POWDER BISCUITS

2 cups flour
3 teaspoons baking
    powder
1 teaspoon salt
3 Tablespoons
    shortening
3/4 cup milk

Sift dry ingredients together. Cut in shortening. Add milk and stir until a soft dough is formed (about 25 strokes). Turn onto lightly floured board and knead until smooth. Roll out (1/2 inch thickness for fluffy biscuits · 1/4 inch for thin, crusty biscuits). Cut with floured cutter. Put biscuits in greased pan.

**Bake 450 degrees —
13-15 minutes.
Makes 12-15 biscuits**

*For "old-time" large fluffy biscuits · the kind Grandma made — pinch off sections of dough and roll by hand.*

# BUTTERMILK BISCUITS

2 cups flour
2-1/2 teaspoons baking
    powder
1/2 teaspoon soda
1 teaspoon salt
2 Tablespoons lard*
1 cup buttermilk
    (more if needed)

Sift dry ingredients together. Cut in lard. Add milk and stir until a soft dough is formed (about 25 strokes). Turn onto lightly floured board and knead until smooth. Roll out (1/2 inch thickness for fluffy biscuits · 1/4 inch for crusty, thin biscuits). Cut with floured cutter. Put biscuits in greased pan.

**Bake 450 degrees —
13-15 minutes.
Makes 12-15 biscuits**

*\*Lard is the rendered fat from a hog. Shortening may be substituted.*

# CHEESE BISCUITS

2 cups flour
3 teaspoons baking
   powder
1 teaspoon salt
1 cup milk
4 Tablespoons
   shortening
3/4 cup grated cheese
1 teaspoon paprika

Sift flour, baking powder and salt together. Cut shortening into dry mixture. Add milk and cheese. Knead gently and quickly. Drop into greased muffin tin or skillet. Sprinkle with paprika before baking.

**Bake 400 degrees — 12 to 15 minutes.
Makes 10-12 biscuits**

# POTATO BISCUITS

1 cup flour
3 teaspoons baking
   powder
1 teaspoon salt
2 Tablespoons bacon
   drippings
1 cup mashed potatoes
1/2 cup milk

Sift dry ingredients, then add potatoes and bacon drippings . Add enough milk to make dough soft. Roll out on floured board 1/2 inch thick. Cut with floured cutter. Place biscuits in greased pan.

**Bake 400 degrees — 12 to 15 minutes.
Makes 10-12 biscuits**

# OLD FASHIONED HOTCAKES

**3 eggs**
**1 teaspoon vanilla**
**1-1/2 cups milk**
**3 Tablespoons butter**
**2-1/2 cups flour**
**2-1/2 teaspoons baking powder**
**4 Tablespoons sugar**

Beat eggs, vanilla and milk together. Add butter (butter should be very soft). Sift all dry ingredients and beat lightly as flour mixture is gradually added. All liquid may not be used to reach pouring consistency needed for fluffy hotcakes. Pour onto hot, oiled griddle. Cook over medium heat until brown on bottom side. Turn and brown on other side.

**Serves 4-6**

*Serve hot with syrup, molasses or jam. A pat of butter may be added between the cakes.*

# BUTTERMILK WAFFLES

3 cups flour
1 teaspoon salt
2-1/2 teaspoons baking
    powder
1 teaspoon soda
4 eggs (separated)
2-1/2 cups buttermilk
7 Tablespoons
    shortening (melted)

Beat egg whites until stiff and set aside. Sift all dry ingredients. Beat egg yolks and add buttermilk and shortening. Add dry ingredients to buttermilk mixture and beat until creamy. Fold in egg whites. Pour into hot waffle iron until golden brown

**Makes 9 large waffles**

*breads*

# CORN BREAD

**2 cups yellow cornmeal**
**4 Tablespoons flour**
**1-1/2 teaspoons baking powder**
**1 teaspoon salt**
**1-1/2 cups buttermilk**
**2 eggs (beaten)**
**2 Tablespoons bacon drippings**

Sift cornmeal, flour, baking powder and salt. Add buttermilk, eggs and bacon drippings. Stir only until all ingredients are mixed well. Pour into greased skillet.

**Bake 400 degrees —**
**approximately 30 minutes.**
**Serves 4-6**

*Slice it, sop it, spoon it, coon it—*
*Be it stick, wedge, dropped, or poured,*
*There's nothing better when served up hot.*
*Pan fried, deep fried, baked or boiled,*
*Mixed with hot water, milk, fat or lard,*
*Eaten with syrup, butter or 'pot-likker' and greens,*
*Crumbled in peas or fresh butter beans,*
*Or try it in milk just before bed,*
*There's nothing better than good old southern cornbread.*

# SPOON BREAD

1 cup cornmeal
3 cups milk
1 teaspoon sugar
1-1/2 teaspoons salt
1 Tablespoon butter
3 eggs (separated)

Scald milk. Gradually add cornmeal and stir until mushy (about 10 minutes). Allow mixture to cool for 5-10 minutes and add salt, beaten egg yolks, butter and sugar. Fold in stiffly beaten egg whites. Pour into greased skillet or baking dish.

**Bake 375 degrees — 35 to 40 minutes.
Serves 4-6**

# BACON CORNBREAD MUFFINS

12 slices bacon
3 eggs
1 cup milk
2 Tablespoons bacon
    drippings
1 cup flour
1 cup cornmeal
2 Tablespoons sugar
3 teaspoons baking
    powder
1/2 teaspoon salt

Fry bacon until crisp, drain and set aside. Mix eggs, milk and fat. Beat mixture with small fork until well mixed (more milk may be added if needed). Sift dry ingredients and add to liquid mixture. Crumble bacon and stir into mixture (do not over-beat). Pour into greased muffin pan.

**Bake 425 degrees — 20 minutes
Makes 12 muffins**

*breads*

# CORN PONE

3 cups cornmeal
2 teaspoons salt
1-1/4 cups boiling
    water
1 teaspoon bacon fat
2 eggs
1 cup cream
2 teaspoons baking
    powder

Mix cornmeal, salt and bacon fat. Pour into boiling water and stir until well mixed. Add eggs and cream. Set aside to cool for 1 hour. Then beat well and add baking powder and pour into greased skillet.
**Bake 400 degrees — 30 to 40 minutes.**
**Serves 4-6**

# FRIED HOT WATER CORNBREAD

2 cups cornmeal
3/4 teaspoon salt
4 cups water
1/2 teaspoon baking
    powder

Bring water to brisk boil in a sauce pan. Mix all dry ingredients. Add 1/2 of water and mix thoroughly. Add more water if needed for thick mixture. Spoon and pat into 1/2 x 3 inch pones and deep fry in very hot fat until brown.
**Serves 5-7**

## COUCHE COUCHE

*(Pronounced cush cush)*

**2-1/4 cups cornmeal**
**1-1/2 teaspoons salt**
**1 teaspoon baking
    powder**
**1 cup cream**
**1/2 cup water**
**2 Tablespoons
    bacon drippings**

Mix dry ingredients. Add cream and water. Heat fat in iron skillet and pour in batter. Lower heat and stir occasionally.
**Cook approximately 15 minutes.**

*Serve as a cereal with sugar and cream.*

## HOE CAKES

**2 cups yellow cornmeal**
**1 cup flour**
**2 teaspoons baking
    powder**
**1 teaspoon salt**
**2 Tablespoons sugar**
**4 Tablespoons bacon
    drippings**
**1 cup milk**

Combine dry ingredients. Mix with one Tablespoon bacon drippings and milk (more milk may be used if needed). Stiff batter is needed to form small, flat cakes. Heat remaining bacon drippings in skillet and fry cakes on medium low heat until brown on both sides. Turn only once.
**Serves 4-6**

*The hoe cake got its name from field workers who cooked small, flat pieces of cornbread on a hoe held over an open fire.*

# HUSH PUPPIES

**2 cups yellow cornmeal**
**1/2 cup flour**
**2 Tablespoons sugar**
**1-1/2 teaspoons salt**
**4-1/2 cups water**
**4 Tablespoons butter**
**1/3 cup parsley (minced)**
**1/3 cup green onions (minced)**
**1/4 cup chopped onion**
**1 Tablespoon hot green peppers (minced)**

Mix all dry ingredients. In a saucepan add water and butter and bring to a boil. Add parsley, onions and peppers. Bring to a brisk boil for approximately 5 minutes or until onions become clear. Gradually add dry ingredients, stirring constantly to prevent lumping. Cook over low heat for 3-5 minutes. Mixture will become thick. Remove from heat and pour into a shallow pan or cookie sheet. Let cool. Roll into slender 3-4 inch lengths.

**Deep fry in hot fat until lightly brown. Serves 8-10**

# RICE CAKES

**1 cup rice (cooked)**
**2 cups cream**
**1-1/2 cups flour**
**1/2 teaspoon salt**
**1-1/4 Tablespoons sugar**
**2 teaspoons baking powder**
**1 egg**
**1 Tablespoon shortening (melted)**

Cover cooked rice with 1 cup cream and let set overnight. Sift dry ingredients. Mix egg, 1 cup cream and shortening in a separate container. Alternating, add small amounts of dry ingredients and liquid mixture into rice and cream. Drop from spoon into a hot greased skillet. Allow to brown on one side, then turn only one time.

**Makes 20-24 cakes**

*Serve warm syrup over the cakes.*

# ANADAMA LOAF BREAD

**5-1/2 to 6-1/2 cups
sifted flour**
**2-1/2 teaspoons salt**
**1 cup yellow cornmeal**
**1/4 cup butter**
**2 cups warm water**
**1/2 cup molasses (room
temperature)**
**2 packages yeast †**

Use a large bowl to mix 2-1/2 cups flour, salt, cornmeal, yeast and softened butter. Slowly add warm water and molasses to dry ingredients. Beat 300 strokes* by hand. Add 1/2 cup of flour (enough to make a thick batter). Beat another 300 strokes. Stir in additional flour to make a soft dough. Turn onto floured board and knead until smooth and elastic (8-10 minutes). Place dough in greased bowl. Cover and let rise in draft free, warm area for 1 hour or until double in size. Punch down dough and turn onto lightly floured board. Divide dough in half and shape into loaves. Put in two greased 9 inch loaf pans. Cover and let rise in warm place until double in bulk (45 minutes).

**Bake 375 degrees — 35 minutes.
Makes 2 loaves**

† *Before the commercial production of yeast, sourdough was the only means of leavening bread.*

*A spry old gentleman, born in 1901, told the following story. "Ma and Pa got married when Ma was thirteen and Pa was twenty. Their folks ' give them ' fifty pounds of cotton seed, three hens, a rooster and a gallon of sourdough for a 'weddin' present."*

* *300 strokes will equal approximately two minutes with mixer on medium speed.*

# WHITE LOAF BREAD

**1 cup milk**
**2 Tablespoons sugar**
**2-1/2 teaspoons salt**
**5 Tablespoons shortening**
**1 cup warm water**
**2 packages dry yeast**
**6 cups flour**

Dissolve yeast in water. Scald milk and stir in salt, sugar and shortening. Allow to cool until lukewarm. Add yeast to milk mixture. Add 3 cups of flour and beat until smooth. Stir in additional flour (the amount of flour used may vary slightly). Turn bread onto a lightly floured board and knead until smooth and elastic. Put in a greased bowl and brush lightly with shortening. Cover and let rise in a warm, draft-free place until dough has doubled in size - usually 30-40 minutes. Turn onto a floured board, punch down and divide in half. Let set for 15-20 minutes. Place in greased 9 inch loaf pans. Cover and let rise for approximately 1 hour.

**Bake 400 degrees — 35 to 40 minutes.**
**Makes 2 loaves**

# SALLY LUNN BREAD

**2 cups flour**
**3 teaspoons baking**
**powder**
**1/2 teaspoon salt**
**4-1/2 Tablespoons**
**shortening**
**1/3 cup sugar**
**2 eggs**
**3/4 cup milk**
**1/2 cup brown sugar**
**(packed firmly)**
**2 teaspoons cinnamon**
**1 Tablespoon butter**
**(melted)**

Sift flour, baking powder and salt together. Cream shortening and sugar thoroughly. Add eggs, one at a time, beating well after each. Add flour, alternately with milk, beating after each is added. Pour into greased 9 inch square pan. Mix brown sugar, cinnamon and butter, sprinkle over the top of batter.

**Bake 400 degrees — 25 minutes.**
**Serves 6-8**

*Sally Lunn is a quick bread used by most of our great-great grandmothers.*

# BLACK WALNUT BREAD

**3 cups flour**
**3 teaspoons baking**
**powder**
**1/4 teaspoon soda**
**1-1/2 teaspoons salt**
**2/3 cup sugar**
**1/4 cup brown sugar**
**1 teaspoon cinnamon**
**2 eggs**
**1-1/4 cups milk**
**2 Tablespoons**
**shortening**
**1 cup black walnuts**
**(finely ground)**

Sift dry ingredients. Combine eggs and milk. Add to flour mixture, cream in shortening just enough to blend all ingredients. Fold in nuts. Pour into 8 inch loaf pan. Let stand at room temperature for 30 minutes.

**Bake 350 degrees — 50 to 60 minutes.**

*Wrap in wax paper and damp towel —wait at least 12 hours after baking to slice when using for finger sandwiches. May also be served warm.*

# SYRUP BREAD

1 teaspoon vanilla
1 cup shortening
1 cup sugar
1 cup cane syrup
5 cups flour
1 teaspoon allspice
1 teaspoon cloves
1 teaspoon ginger
1 teaspoon cinnamon
1 cup water
3 teaspoons baking
    soda

Mix together vanilla, shortening, sugar and syrup. In another bowl mix flour, allspice, cloves, ginger and cinnamon. Boil water and add baking soda. Combine the first two mixtures and gradually add water and stir until all mixtures are well blended. Pour into 15x10½x1-inch pan.

**Bake 350 degrees — 20 to 25 minutes.**
**Serves 6-8**

*To make fruit bars, add raisins and make a mixture of 1 egg and 2 Tablespoons water. Brush over dough before baking. After bread is baked, make a glaze of powdered sugar and cooking oil and brush lightly while still warm.*

# PUMPKIN BREAD

**3 cups flour**
**1 teaspoon baking**
**    powder**
**1 teaspoon salt**
**2 teaspoons cinnamon**
**1/2 teaspoon nutmeg**
**1/4 teaspoon ground**
**    cloves**
**2 eggs (beaten)**
**1-1/4 cups pumpkin**
**    (cooked)**
**1 cup milk**
**1 cup brown sugar**
**1 teaspoon baking**
**    soda**
**1/2 cup cooking oil**
**1 cup pecans**

Sift flour, baking powder, salt, cinnamon, nutmeg and cloves together. In another bowl, mix eggs, pumpkin, milk, sugar, baking soda and oil. Gradually add flour mixture and fold in pecans. Pour into loaf pan.

**Bake 350 degrees - 1 hour/ten minutes.**
**Makes 2 loaves**

# GINGERBREAD

**1-1/4 cups flour**
**1 teaspoon baking**
 **powder**
**1/4 teaspoon soda**
**1/2 teaspoon salt**
**1 teaspoon cinnamon**
**1/4 teaspoon cloves**
**1/2 teaspoon ginger**
**1/2 cup molasses**
**1/2 cup water**
**3 Tablespoons**
 **shortening**
**5 Tablespoons sugar**
**2 eggs**

Sift flour. Add baking powder, soda, salt and spices. Combine molasses and water. Cream shortening and sugar. Add eggs. Alternately mix dry ingredients with liquid mixture. Beat after each addition until smooth. Bake in 8 inch square pan.

**Bake 350 degrees — 35 minutes.**
**Serves 5-7**

# APPLE BREAD

3 cups flour
1 Tablespoon baking
  powder
1 teaspoon salt
3/4 cup sugar
2 teaspoons cinnamon
3 eggs
1-1/2 cups milk
1 cup pecans (chopped)
1-1/4 cups raisins
1 cup apples (chopped)

Peel and chop apples into small pieces. Combine dry ingredients. Beat eggs and milk. Add flour, baking powder, salt, sugar and cinnamon. Fold in nuts, raisins and apples. Turn into floured loaf pan.

**Bake 375 degrees — 1 hour.**

*For a child growing up in the rural South during The Depression, fruits, nuts and raisins were probably the most common items received at Christmas time. "Tumpie," who is now sixty-one, recalls, "I always believed in Santa Claus until I was eight years old. One Christmas Eve I hid behind the door to get a look at Santa and see if he had brought me the red wagon that I had seen in a catalog. Didn't have to wait long - in the dim light, coming from the fireplace, I saw a familiar weathered old hand reach through the window and carefully place two apples, a handful of walnuts, two boxes of raisins and a home-made rol-pol doll next to the fireplace. There was no mistaking that hand - it was Poppa, my beloved grandfather."*

# HUCKLEBERRY MUFFINS

**2 cups flour**
**3 teaspoons baking
      powder**
**3/4 cup  sugar**
**1 teaspoon salt**
**1/4 cup shortening**
**2 eggs (beaten)**
**1 cup milk**
**1 cup huckleberries**

Sift together all dry ingredients. Blend in shortening and add eggs. Add remaining ingredients using as few strokes as possible. Fold in huckleberries last. Fill greased muffin pans 2/3 full.

**Bake 400 degrees — 25 minutes.**
**Makes 10-12 muffins**

*Blueberries may be substituted.*

# SUGAR MUFFINS

**2 cups flour**
**3 teaspoons baking**
    **powder**
**4 Tablespoons sugar**
**3/4 teaspoon salt**
**1/3 cup shortening**
**1 egg**
**3/4 cup milk**
**1/4 cup butter (melted)**
**2 teaspoons cinnamon**

Mix all dry ingredients, except 2 Tablespoons sugar and cinnamon. Blend in shortening until mixture is coarse in texture. Beat in egg until dough is thoroughly moistened. Fill greased muffin tins 2/3 full.

**Bake 450 degrees — 20 minutes.**

For a sugar-crusted top, remove from tin as soon as muffins are baked and dip muffin tops into melted butter. Drop into a bag containing a mixture of 2 Tablespoons sugar and 2 teaspoons cinnamon and shake.

**Makes 10-12 muffins**

*Serve hot.*

33

# CINNAMON RICE MUFFINS

1-1/2 cups flour
1/4 teaspoon salt
4 Tablespoons sugar
3 teaspoons baking
    powder
1 cup rice (cooked)
3 teaspoons cinnamon
1 cup milk
3 eggs
2 Tablespoons
    shortening

Sift flour, salt, sugar and baking powder. Combine with rice, cinnamon, milk, eggs and shortening. Pour into greased muffin tins.

**Bake 400 degrees - 25 minutes.**
**Makes 10-12 muffins**

**vegetables**

# AFTER THE PICKIN'

Holding a bucket in one hand while standing delicately balanced on one foot, and reaching across two rows of peas for a cluster of choice crowders, would surely qualify for a name more noble than 'pea pickin.' The exercise may have added years to the lives of many, but exercise was not looked upon as the activity of the day. A well-supplied larder was more in favor than well-formed biceps.

Peas, beans, tomatoes, okra, squash, eggplant, onions and a variety of other vegetables and fruits were grown in the garden. It was a daily chore in late spring and summer to harvest the produce. Vegetables had to be picked when they ripened and nature controlled the clock. If there were more than needed for daily use, the surplus was picked and canned for winter when fresh vegetables were not available.

Canning day started early in the morning and often lasted until late evening. The vegetables had to be picked, shelled and washed. Jars had to be cleaned and sterilized and the woodbox filled with adequate firewood for the stove.

Sleep came easy after a long day of canning. The melody of lids snapping as jars of the canned goods cooled and sealed was very soothing as we drifted off to sleep. It had been a good day - but tomorrow is another and there are still three empty shelves remaining in the pantry behind the fireplace.

# AUNT FANELLA'S
# LIMA BEANS AND SAUSAGE

**4 cups shelled fresh lima beans**

**2 cups sliced smoked sausage**

**3/4 cup onion (finely chopped)**

**2 Tablespoons bacon drippings**

**1 teaspoon salt**

**1/2 teaspoon black pepper**

Put beans in 3 quart pot and cover with water. Bring to boil and cook until beans are tender. While beans are cooking, put bacon drippings, onion and sausage in skillet and cook over medium heat until light brown. When beans are tender add sausage, onion, salt and pepper to boiling beans.

**Cook on medium heat — 10 minutes. Serves 4-6**

*Aunt Fanella's recipe has been revised for smaller families.*

*Aunt Fanella is the oldest of nine girls. Growing up in a large family meant having to assume family responsibilites at an early age. While attending school in Delcambre, Louisiana, she met and later married her husband, Clarence. Fanella and Clarence, married for almost 60 years, have twelve children. There is always a "Gathering Up" when children, grandchildren and other relatives visit.*

*While raising her family, Aunt Fanella always followed a disciplined daily schedule. Her day started promptly at 5:00 A.M. with preparation of the family breakfast. With a family of twelve, dinner was started shortly thereafter.*

*Gardening was one of her favorite activities. She could always reach under the bed and pull out the "makings" to cook for a crowd. Her canned goods kept well there because of the coolness in summer and warmth in winter.*

# HONEY BEETS

**4 Tablespoons butter**
**2 Tablespoons mustard**
**1/2 teaspoon salt**
**1/2 teaspoon paprika**
**2 Tablespoons honey**
**2 teaspoons**
 **Worcestershire**
 **sauce**
**3-1/2 cups beets**
 **(cooked)**

Mix all ingredients in a saucepan, except beets. Bring to a brisk boil then add beets.

**Cook on low heat for approximately 5 minutes or until thoroughly heated. Serves 5-7**

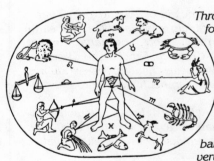

*Through the years, a combination of folklore and interpretations from the almanac has been used to determine the most desirable time to carry out various farm chores. The almanac provides a guide for each day of the month through the twelve signs of the zodiac. All twelve signs appear for two or three days in each month. The signs are known as earthy, dry, barren, moist, watery, fiery, airy, fruitful, very fruitful and feminine or masculine.*

# HOME STYLE CABBAGE

1 head cabbage
(shredded)
2 pounds ham hocks
1/4 cup water
1 Tablespoon red
vinegar
1/2 teaspoon salt
3/4 teaspoon pepper

Bring water to boil. Add all ingredients. Cover and stir occasionally. Cook until cabbage is tender. Additional water may be added if needed.

**Cook over low heat approximately 25 minutes.**
**Serves 4-6**

# FRIED CABBAGE

1 medium cabbage
1 Tablespoon butter
2 teaspoons salt
4 eggs
4 Tablespoons milk
2-1/4 cups flour
1/2 teaspoon pepper
1/4 teaspoon red
pepper

Cut cabbage into 6-8 squares or wedges. Cover with water and add 1 teaspoon salt and 1 Tablespoon butter. Bring to boil for 5-7 minutes. Drain cabbage. Beat eggs and 4 Tablespoons milk. In another container mix flour, pepper and remaining salt. Dip cabbage in egg mixture and coat with flour.

**Deep fry in hot bacon drippings.**
**May also be pan fried.**

**Serves 6-8**

39

*vegetables*

# CABBAGE ROLLS

1 head cabbage
1 pound ground pork
   sausage
2 Tablespoons onion
   (chopped)
1-1/4 cups rice
   (cooked)
2 eggs
1/2 teaspoon salt
1/2 teaspoon pepper
1-1/4 cups tomato
   sauce
1 cup water
3 pounds ham hocks

Wash head of cabbage and drop into boiling water for five minutes. Remove from water and allow to drain. Add onion, rice, eggs, salt and pepper to sausage. Roll the meat mixture in cabbage leaves and secure with a toothpick. Place the ham hocks in the bottom of a cast iron pot with enough water to cover the bottom. Place cabbage rolls over ham hocks. Make a mixture of tomato sauce and 1 cup water. Pour over cabbage rolls.

**Cover and cook over medium low heat approximately 1 hour.**
**Serves 4-6**

# GLAZED HONEY CARROTS

**3 cups sliced carrots**
**1-1/2 cups water**
**1/2 cup honey**
**3 Tablespoons butter**
**1-1/2 teaspoons lemon juice**
**3/4 teaspoon salt**

Add salt to water and bring to a brisk boil. Add carrots and bring back to boil. Add remaining ingredients and reduce to low heat. Cover and cook until tender.

**Serves 4-6**

# BAKED CORN

**2 cups corn (cooked)**
**3 Tablespoons butter**
**1 Tablespoon onion (chopped)**
**1 Tablespoon green pepper**
**2 Tablespoons flour**
**3/4 cup milk**
**3 eggs (separated)**
**1/2 teaspoon vinegar**
**1 teaspoon salt**
**1/2 teaspoon pepper**
**4 Tablespoons bread crumbs**

Melt butter in skillet and brown onion and green pepper. Add flour and gradually stir in milk. Stir until thick and smooth. Add egg yolks, corn, vinegar, salt and pepper. Fold in beaten egg whites. Top with bread crumbs.

**Bake 400 degrees — 20-30 minutes. Serves 4-6**

*"Signs of Planting"*

— *The time to plant corn is when doves begin to coo.*

— *If a wind blows from the south on February 14th, go ahead and plant corn. The crop will not freeze.*

# CREAMY CORN

2 cups creamed corn
1 Tablespoon baking
    powder
3/4 cup cornmeal
1/2 teaspoon salt
4 eggs
1/2 cup bacon
    drippings
3 hot peppers
    (finely chopped)
1 cup grated cheese

Mix all ingredients and pour into lightly greased dish.
**Bake 350 degrees — 45 minutes.**
**Serves 4-6**

# 'ROS-A-NEARS'

*(roasting ears)*

5 ears (fresh corn)
3/4 cup butter
    (softened)
1/2 teaspoon salt
1/2 teaspoon paprika
1/4 teaspoon pepper
1 Tablespoon milk
12 corn shucks

Remove shucks and silk from corn. Save the corn shucks to wrap corn while baking. Soak shucks in warm water for 10 minutes. Mix butter, salt, paprika and milk together to make a creamy paste. Spread the mixture over the ears of corn. Remove shucks from water and drain. Wrap corn in shucks and place in a heavy pot.
**Cover and bake 400 degrees —
30-40 minutes or until tender.**
**Serves 5**

# EGGPLANT CASSEROLE

2 medium eggplants

1-1/2 pounds ground beef

3 Tablespoons bacon drippings

3 Tablespoons onion (chopped)

3 Tablespoons green pepper (chopped)

3 small hot peppers (chopped)

1 teaspoon garlic (chopped)

1-1/2 teaspoons salt

1/4 teaspoon pepper

1-1/2 cups rice (cooked)

2 teaspoons lemon juice

Peel and chop eggplants. Heat fat in skillet. Add eggplant, ground beef, onion, peppers, garlic, salt and pepper. Cook on medium heat, stirring constantly, for 10 minutes or until eggplant begins to tender.Stir in rice. Put into greased baking dish.

**Bake 375 degrees — 30 minutes. Remove from oven and sprinkle with lemon juice. Serves 5-7**

# FRIED EGGPLANT

**1 medium eggplant**
**4 cups water**
**1 teaspoon salt**
**1/2 teaspoon pepper**
**2 eggs**
**1/2 cup milk**
**3/4 cup flour**

Peel and slice eggplant into thin strips. Soak in 1/2 teaspoon salt and 4 cups water for 30 minutes. Remove eggplant from water and drain. Add remaining salt and pepper. Let set for 10 minutes. Mix eggs and milk for batter. Dip eggplant into batter and roll in flour.

**Fry in one inch fat until golden brown.**

# MUSTARD GREENS AND HAM HOCKS

**1 mess\* mustard greens**
**1-1/2 pounds ham**
**    hocks**
**2 cups water**
**salt and pepper to taste**
**1 Tablespoon cane**
**    syrup**

Wash greens thoroughly. Brown ham hocks in skillet with 1 Tablespoon fat. Put greens in pot and add water. Add ham hocks. Cover and cook on medium low heat for 30 minutes. Add salt and syrup. Cover and cook another 10-15 minutes.
**Serves 4-6**

*Serve with cornbread.*

# COUNTRY COLLARDS

Clean and wash 1 mess\* collard greens. Chop leaves into thirds. Put collards in a 4 quart boiler. Add 4 cups water, 1-1/2 teaspoons sugar, 1 teaspoon salt and 1-1/2 pounds ham hocks. Bring to boil. Reduce heat to slow boil. Cover and cook until tender.

*\*Mess — any measured amount of vegetables or meat necessary to serve a given number of people.*

# BAKED GRITS*

1 cup grits
4-1/4 cups water
1/2 cup butter
3/4 cup cheese
3 eggs
3/4 cup milk
1 teaspoon salt
1/4 teaspoon red
    pepper

Cook grits in 4-1/4 cups salted water. As grits begin to thicken, add butter and cheese. Beat eggs and milk and add to grit mixture. Pour into baking dish.
**Bake 350 degrees — 25 minutes.**
**Serves 8-10**

*Grits are made from coarsely ground corn. This is a favored breakfast food in the South.

# FRIED OKRA

8 pods okra
1 cup cornmeal (yellow)
1 Tablespoon flour
1-1/2 teaspoons salt
1/2 teaspoon pepper

Slice okra into 1/4 inch slices. Sprinkle okra with cold water. Mix all dry ingredients. Coat okra thoroughly with cornmeal mixture. Remove okra from mixture.

**Deep fry in 1-2 inches bacon drippings until golden brown.**
**Serves 4-6**

# PICKLED OKRA

6 pounds okra
12 cloves garlic
12 pods hot pepper
12 teaspoons celery
    seed
12 teaspoons dill seed
1 cup salt (not iodized)
2 cups sugar
2 quarts water
2 quarts vinegar (white)

Wash okra and pack in 12 sterilized pint jars. Put equal amounts of garlic, hot pepper, celery seed, and dill seed in jars. Combine sugar, salt, water and vinegar in pot and bring to boil. Pour liquid into jars. Cap jars and cover with hot water for ten minutes.

**Makes 12 pints**

*"Signs of Planting"*
*— Never plant on the 1st day*
*of a New Moon.*

# PEAS N' OKRA

**4 cups fresh field peas**
**4-1/2 cups water**
**1 Tablespoon salt**
**1/4 teaspoon black**
**pepper**
**1/4 pound salt pork**
**1 teaspoon sugar**
**(optional)**
**8 pods okra**

Pour water into pot, and add all ingredients, except okra. Cover and cook over medium heat for 30 minutes, add pods of okra and cook for approximately 15 additional minutes or until vegetables are tender.

**Serves 4-7**

# FRIED PEA FRITTERS

**2 cups cooked field**
**peas**
**1 cup flour**
**2 teaspoons baking**
**powder**
**1 teaspoon pepper**
**1/2 teaspoon salt**
**1 Tablespoon curry**
**powder**
**2 eggs**
**1-1/2 cups milk**

Mix all dry ingredients. Beat eggs and milk. Add to the flour mixture. Gently stir in cooked peas. Drop from spoon into 3/4 inch hot fat.

**Fry until light brown.**
**Serves 4-5**

*"Signs of Planting"*
*— Plant on "Bloom Day" and the harvest will be light. Plants will have more blooms and vines than fruits.*

# 'POKE SALAD'

Pick when plants are young and tender. *Do not eat poke after it has bloomed and has berries.* Wash thoroughly. Put in pot with enough water to cover. Boil for 5 minutes. Drain and replace with hot boiling water. Boil for an additional 5 minutes. Drain and put into heavy skillet with 6 Tablespoons bacon drippings. Add 1 finely chopped onion. Cover and simmer until onions are tender. Beat 5 eggs until foamy and scramble with greens and onion. Salt and pepper to taste.

# FRIED IRISH POTATOES

4 large potatoes
1 cup flour
1 teaspoon salt
1/2 teaspoon pepper
1/2 teaspoon paprika

Slice potatoes into 1/2 inch strips and cover with water. Combine flour, salt, pepper and paprika. Put mixture into small paper bag. Remove potatoes from water, but do not blot. Drop a few slices at a time into the bag and shake. Deep fry in hot grease.
**Serves 6-8**

# HOMEMADE "POTATO CHIPS"

Using only large or medium potatoes, peel and slice into very, very thin wafers. Soak in ice water for two hours. Remove from water. Drain and sprinkle with salt - (1/2 teaspoon salt per cup of potatoes). Drop potatoes in hot grease (a few slices at a time). Keep potatoes circulating in grease until golden brown. Drain and season with red pepper if desired.

*"Planting Signs"*
*— Potatoes planted when signs are in the feet will not be smooth, but will have little "toes" grow all over the potatoes.*

# STUFFED IRISH POTATOES

5 large potatoes
   (baked)
1 Tablespoon butter
2 Tablespoons cream
1 Tablespoon green
   onion (chopped)
1-1/2 cups ground beef
2 teaspoons
   Worcestershire
   sauce
1/2 cup cheese (grated)
1/4 teaspoon salt
1/4 teaspoon red
   pepper
1/4 teaspoon paprika

Cut a thin lengthwise slice from side of baked potato. Scoop out inside of potato without breaking skin. Mix all ingredients, except cheese and paprika, with the scooped out portion. Do not mash potato mixture. Place stuffed potatoes in open baking dish. Sprinkle with cheese and paprika.

**Bake 350 degrees — 25 minutes.
Serves 5**

*Small amounts of milk or beef stock may be used to moisten potato mixture before baking should mixture be too dry.*

# POTATOES AND CREAM

**4 medium white
   potatoes**
**1/2 small onion**
**5 Tablespoons butter**
**2-1/2 Tablespoons flour**
**3/4 teaspoon salt**
**1/2 teaspoon pepper**
**2 cups cream**
**1/2 cup bread crumbs**

Slice potatoes and onions into thin round slices. Melt 3 Tablespoons butter in skillet. Add flour, salt, and pepper. Gradually add cream, stirring constantly until sauce thickens. Layer a baking dish with potatoes and onions. Pour sauce over a layer of potatoes and continue to alternate layers of potatoes with sauce. Take remaining butter and mix with bread crumbs to make a crust.

**Cover and bake 300 degrees
— 30 minutes.**

# POTATO PATTIES

**2 cups leftover mashed
 potatoes**
**2 teaspoons green
 onions (chopped)**
**1 egg**
**1/4 teaspoon salt**
**1/4 teaspoon pepper**
**1/2 teaspoon paprika**
**1/2 cup grated cheese**
**2 Tablespoons butter**

Combine all ingredients except butter. Heat 2 Tablespoons of butter in a skillet. Make small balls of the potato mixture. Brown in butter and serve hot.

**Serves 4-6**

*"Signs of Planting"*
*— Plant potatoes during the
dark nights of March.*

# PERFECT RICE

1 cup rice
2 cups water
1 teaspoon salt
1 Tablespoon butter

Add salt and butter to boiling water. Stir in rice and bring to boil. Cover and reduce heat as low as possible. Do not stir or open lid while cooking.

**Cook approximately 20 minutes.**

# GREEN RICE

3/4 cup green onions
    (minced)
3 teaspoons olive oil
1/2 cup green pepper
    (minced)
1 cup celery
    (chopped)
1 cup rice
2 bay leaves
2 cups chicken broth
1 teaspoon salt
1/4 teaspoon pepper
3/4 teaspoon curry
    powder

Cook onions in olive oil until soft, but not brown. Add remaining ingredients. Pour into a 2 quart baking dish and cover.

**Bake 350 degrees — 45 minutes.**

# SPICY GREEN BEANS

**2 Tablespoons bacon
    drippings**
**2 Tablespoons flour**
**1 Tablespoon brown
    sugar**
**1/2 teaspoon salt**
**1-1/2 Tablespoons
    vinegar**
**1/2 teaspoon cinnamon**
**3 cups green beans
    (cooked)**

Heat bacon drippings in skillet. Stir in flour until mixture is smooth. Add remainder of ingredients and cover.

**Simmer over medium low heat — 15 minutes.**
**Serves 4-6**

# STUFFED SQUASH

**3 squash (yellow)**
**2-1/2 cups water**
**2 teaspoons salt**
**1 Tablespoon bacon
   drippings**
**1 garlic clove (crushed)**
**1/2 pound ground beef**
**1/2 cup rice (uncooked)**
**1/2 teaspoon pepper**
**2 cups tomatoes
   (stewed)**

### SAUCE

**2 Tablespoons butter**
**2 Tablespoons flour**
**1/2 teaspoon dry
   mustard**
**1/4 teaspoon salt**
**1/4 teaspoon red
   pepper**
**1 cup milk**
**1/4 cup cheese**

Cut squash lengthwise. Scrape out seeds. Add two cups water and 1 teaspoon salt into a heavy pot with tight fitting lid. Bring to boil. Add squash with sliced side down and cook over medium heat for 5 minutes or until tender. Remove squash and let drain. Heat bacon drippings in a heavy skillet. Add garlic and ground beef. Cook until browned (approximately 10 minutes). Add rice, salt, pepper, tomatoes and 1/2 cup water. Cover and cook over low heat for approximately 20 minutes, or until liquid is absorbed. Fill squash halves with mixture and arrange in bottom of baking pan.

### Sauce

Melt butter in a saucepan. Stir in flour, mustard, salt, pepper and milk. Bring to a boil, stirring until thickened. Reduce heat and add cheese. Cook slowly until cheese is melted and mixture is smooth. Pour 1/2 of cheese sauce over squash. Bake 15 to 20 minutes. Add remainder of sauce before serving.

**Serves 6**

# FRIED SQUASH

**3 large squash (white)**
**2 eggs (beaten)**
**1/2 cup milk**
**2 cups buttered bread crumbs**
**salt and pepper to taste**

Peel and slice squash into thin slices. Salt and pepper to taste. Dip squash into mixture of eggs and milk. Roll in bread crumbs and dip in milk a second time. Roll squash in bread crumbs and drop into hot grease until brown (approximately 5 minutes).

**Serves 4-6**

# SQUASH AND CHEESE DISH

**1 pound squash**
**(yellow)**
**2 cups water**
**1 small onion**
**1 cup cheese**
**(grated)**
**1 Tablespoon butter**
**1/2 cup bread crumbs**
**1 cup milk**
**2 eggs (separated)**
**1/2 teaspoon salt**
**1/2 teaspoon pepper**

Slice squash and chop onion. Cook in 2 cups water until tender. Drain, add butter and mash thoroughly. Add cheese, milk, bread crumbs, egg yolks, salt and pepper. Allow to cool. Fold in stiffly beaten egg whites. Pour into greased baking dish.

**Bake 350 degrees — until lightly browned.**
**Serves 4-6**

# STUFFED SWEET POTATO

**7 - 8 medium sweet potatoes**
**4 Tablespoons bacon drippings**
**1 cup cheese (grated)**
**4 Tablespoons butter**
**8 slices bacon (fried)**

Wash and grease the skins of the potatoes. Bake at 350 degree for one hour or until soft. Cut slice from top of each potato. Scoop out inside of potato being careful to avoid breaking shell. Mix cheese, butter and scooped out potato. Fold in crisp fried bacon. Scoop mixture back into shell. **Bake 350 degrees — for 30-35 minutes.**
**Serves 7**

# FRIED SWEET POTATOES

Slice uncooked sweet potatoes thin and crosswise. Drop slices into hot grease and fry until browned. Sprinkle with salt, sugar or cinnamon.

Leftover baked sweet potatoes can be sliced into 1 inch thick slices and pan fried in butter or bacon drippings. Sprinkle with cinnamon or sugar.

*"Signs of Planting"*
*— If there is thunder at night in February, beware of a cold spell in April.*

# YUMMY SWEET POTATOES

**3 cups sweet potatoes
    (baked)**
**1/4 cup sugar**
**1 Tablespoon vanilla**
**8 Tablespoons butter
    (melted)**
**2 eggs**
**3/4 cup brown sugar**
**1/3 cup flour**
**1 cup pecans
    (chopped)**

Mash potatoes and add sugar, vanilla, 4 Tablespoons butter and eggs. Pour into baking dish. Top with a mixture of brown sugar, flour, pecans and 4 Tablespoons butter. Sprinkle over potatoes.
**Bake 350 degrees — 25 minutes.**

# SWEET POTATO BAKE

6 sweet potatoes
1-1/4 cups butter
pinch of salt
2 teaspoons cinnamon
1 cup brown sugar
1/2 teaspoon vanilla
1/2 teaspoon nutmeg
1/3 cup apricot brandy
1 cup pecans (chopped)
14 large marshmallows

Grease skin of potatoes and bake in shallow tin 325 degrees until soft. Allow potatoes to cool. Peel, mash and add all remaining ingredients, except pecans. Beat mixture until smooth. Put into baking dish and refrigerate overnight. Bake 350 degrees for 25 minutes. Remove potatoes from oven. Fold in pecans and top with marshmallows. Bake 10-12 minutes or until marshmallows are slightly browned.

**Serves 6-8**

# TURNIP GREENS

Wash 2 bunches of turnip greens thoroughly. Chop greens into small pieces. Put greens in pot with 4 cups water. More water may be used if necessary. Add 1-1/2 teaspoons sugar, 1 teaspoon salt, 1/2 teaspoon pepper and 1/4 pound salt pork. Bring to brisk boil. Reduce heat to medium low. Cover and cook until tender.

# TURNIP ROOTS

**4 turnip (roots)**
**1-1/2 cups water**
**1/4 teaspoon salt**
**1/4 teaspoon pepper**
**1 teaspoon sugar**
   **(optional)**
**2 slices salt pork**

Slice turnips 1/4 inch thick. Combine turnips, water, salt, pepper, sugar and salt meat in a heavy pot. Cover and cook on high heat for 5 minutes. Reduce heat to medium low and cook for 30 minutes or until tender.

*"Signs of Planting"*

*— Never plant when signs are in the heart or head. These are "death signs."*

# FRIED TOMATOES

**3 tomatoes**
    **(firm or unripened)**
**2 cups cornmeal**
**1 teaspoon salt**
**1/2 teaspoon pepper**
**1/2 teaspoon paprika**
**1 Tablespoon flour**

Slice tomatoes into thick crosswise slices. Combine all dry ingredients. Coat tomatoes with dry mixture. Drop into hot fat until golden brown.

**Serves 4-6**

# CHILI SAUCE

**22 large tomatoes**
**4 onions**
**3 bell peppers**
**4 sweet peppers**
**4 hot peppers**
**2 Tablespoons dry**
**      mustard**
**2 teaspoons nutmeg**
**2 teaspoons cinnamon**
**1 teaspoon cloves**
**1 teaspoon ginger**
**3/4 cup sugar**
**2 Tablespoons salt**
**4-1/2 cups vinegar**

Peel tomatoes and onions. Chop all vegetables. Add spices, sugar, vinegar and salt. Cook on low heat until mixture thickens. Must be stirred frequently to prevent sticking. Pack into hot sterilized jars and seal.

*Amounts of salt, hot peppers and sugar may be changed according to taste.*

# CHOW CHOW

**20 green tomatoes**
**9 cucumbers**
**6 small onions**
**1 green bell pepper**
**1 bunch celery**
**3 red peppers**
**1 pound snap beans**
**1/2 cup salt**
**2 quarts vinegar**
**2 Tablespoons turmeric**
**1 cup brown sugar**
**4 Tablespoons mustard seed**
**1 Tablespoon cloves**
**1 Tablespoon pepper**

Peel and dice tomatoes, cucumbers and onions. Chop peppers, snap beans and celery. Mix all vegetables together. Arrange vegetables in layers. Sprinkle each layer with salt. Let stand 24 hours. Drain and combine vinegar, sugar and spices. Heat to boiling, stirring frequently. Simmer until vegetables are tender. Pack in hot sterilized jars and seal.

# CRISP PICKLE SLICES

**4 quarts medium cucumbers (sliced)**

**6 medium white onions (chopped)**

**2 green peppers (chopped)**

**3 garlic cloves**

**1/3 cup salt**

**5 cups sugar**

**3 cups cider vinegar**

**1-1/2 teaspoons turmeric**

**1-1/2 teaspoons celery seed**

**2 Tablespoons mustard seed**

Do not pare cucumbers. Slice thin. Add onions, peppers and whole garlic cloves. Add salt and cover with cracked ice. Mix thoroughly. Let stand 3 hours. Drain well and combine remaining ingredients. Pour over cucumber mixture. Heat just to a boil. Seal in hot sterilized jars.

# GREEN TOMATO PICKLES

**10 pounds green tomatoes**

**2/3 cup salt**

**6 cups water**

**4-1/2 pounds onions (white)**

**4 cups vinegar**

**1 cup sugar**

**2 Tablespoons mustard seed**

**2 Tablespoons celery seed**

Slice tomatoes and onions. Place tomatoes and onions in a large crock alternating a layer of each. Sprinkle each layer with salt. Cover and let set overnight. Drain and add 2 cups vinegar and 2 cups water. Heat to boiling. Drain and add 2 cups vinegar, 4 cups water, sugar, celery seed and mustard seed. Bring to a slow boil for thirty minutes. Stir occasionally. Pack into hot sterilized jars.

**soups**

**salads**

**gravies**

## GATHERING POKE

Nothing creates a craving for fresh greens like a long, cold winter or an extended diet of dried beans. The geese have all gone back North. The ham and middlings that hung in the smokehouse have been eaten. All that remains is salty fat back.

Early mornings are still cool. But with the sun glistening on a heavy dew and young leaves shimmering in a gentle breeze, there is no doubt that the hunger for a change of diet can be satisfied.

Even Junior, who usually puts up a fuss about such chores, is easily persuaded to grab a bucket and head for the fence lines. That's where 'Poke Salad' grows.

Those tender young leaves boiled down with a strip of salt pork are the next best thing to spring turnip greens. Nothing is wasted when there is fried hot water bread to crumble in a bowl and cover with 'pot-likker' from the bottom of the pot.

# AUNT EUNICE'S GARDEN SOUP

**1 Tablespoon butter**
**5 carrots (diced)**
**4 turnips (diced)**
**3/4 cup cabbage**
**3 green onions**
**(chopped)**
**8 cups soup stock**
**1-1/2 cups peas**
**(shelled)**
**salt and pepper to taste**
**4 potatoes (diced)**
**3 Tablespoons parsley**
**(minced)**

In a heavy pot, melt butter and add carrots, turnips and cabbage. Saute lightly. Add soup stock, onions, peas, potatoes, parsley, salt and pepper. Simmer for 40 minutes.

**Serves 6-8**

> *Aunt Eunice is one of Fanella's younger sisters. And like the rest of the family she is an excellent cook. While growing up along the bayous of South Louisiana, she learned to take a little salt, a lot of pepper and whatever else that was in the kitchen and prepare a delicious meal. Add a skillet of bread and Eunice's day in the kitchen was over, with plenty of seconds for everyone. She still relies on these one pot meals to give extra time for her favorite entertainment — playing cards.*

# BEEF BOUILLON

**2-1/2 pounds beef (stew)**
**2 quarts water**
**1/2 cup celery**
**1/2 cup onion**
**1/2 cup carrots**
**1 clove**
**1 teaspoon salt**
**1/4 teaspoon pepper**

Cube meat and cover with water. Add salt and bring to boil. Cover and simmer for two hours. Add remainder of ingredients and simmer approximately 1 hour. Add additional water if needed. Strain and allow to cool. Skim excess fat. Heat and serve hot.

**Serves 6**

*To clarify the beef bouillon pour into pot while cold. Stir in 1-2 slightly beaten egg whites. Heat and stir until liquid boils. Set aside for ten minutes. Strain through a cheesecloth.*

*"Home Remedies" were concocted for aches, ailments and imperfections of all kinds. These remedies were used with unrelenting faith that proper application would remove or alleviate a given problem. Brewed teas, soups from special herbs, boiled roots, poultices from tree bark were but a few of the gifts of nature used "to cure."*

# CHICKEN AND RICE SOUP

**1 medium chicken
(2 to 2-1/2 pounds)
5 cups water
salt and pepper to taste
1 cup rice**

Cut chicken into small pieces and season with salt and pepper. Let set for ten minutes. Put chicken into heavy pot and add water. Cover and cook on medium heat until chicken is tender (approximately 1 hour). Remove chicken from broth, debone and skim excess fat from the top. Bring broth to brisk boil. Add chicken and rice. Season to taste. Cover and reduce heat. **Simmer — approximately 20 minutes.**

*Additional water may be added.*

soups

# HAM AND BEAN SOUP

**2 cups dry lima beans**
**1 onion (chopped)**
**2 cups ham**
**(cooked and cubed)**
**1 cup corn (cooked)**
**3 slices bacon**
**1-1/2 Tablespoons flour**
**salt and pepper to taste**

Fry bacon in heavy skillet. Drain and crumble. Keep drippings for later use. Cover beans with water in a heavy pot. Bring to boil. Cook until beans are tender approximately 2-1/2 hours. Add onion, seasoning, ham, corn and bacon. Simmer for 1 hour. In a small skillet, add bacon drippings, flour and stir until lightly browned. Add 1-1/2 cups water to make a gravy, stirring frequently. Pour into soup and simmer for 25 to 30 minutes.
**Serves 4-6**

# OKRA SOUP

**4 cups okra**
**1 ham bone**
**1 cup celery**
**1/2 green pepper**
  **(chopped)**
**1/2 onion (chopped)**
**4 Tablespoons bacon**
  **drippings**
**4 tomatoes (ripe)**
**1 teaspoon salt**
**1 teaspoon brown sugar**
**6 cups boiling water**

Slice okra and celery crosswise. Chop green pepper and onion. Brown in fat for approximately five minutes. Put ham bone in a heavy pot and cover with water. Add browned pepper and onion. Boil until meat separates from bone. Cut tomatoes into quarters. Add all ingredients.

**Simmer — approximately 1 hour.**
**Serves 5**

# OYSTER STEW

**1/4 cup butter**
**1 pint oysters**
   **(with liquid)**
**1 cup milk**
**1/2 cup cream**
**1/2 teaspoon salt**
**1/4 teaspoon pepper**
**1/8 teaspoon paprika**

Pour oysters and liquid into a saucepan. Bring to a brisk boil until edges of oysters begin to shrivel and curl. Add butter and stir until melted. Reduce to medium heat. Add milk and cream (curdling will occur only if milk is beginning to sour). Season with salt and pepper. Increase heat and bring to light boil. Spinkle with paprika and serve hot.

**Serves 4**

*When using fresh oysters, one cup water may be used for liquid.*

# PIG'S FEET SOUP

**1-1/2 pounds pig's feet**
**2 cups water**
**2 teaspoons salt**
**1/4 teaspoon ginger**
**1/4 teaspoon**
    **red pepper**
**1-1/2 pounds squash**
    **(cubed)**
**2 tomatoes (chopped)**
**1 cup lima beans**
    **(cooked)**

Add pig's feet, salt, ginger and pepper to boiling water. Cover and simmer for 1-1/2 hours. In another pot boil squash until tender. Remove, drain and mash squash. Add squash, tomatoes and lima beans to soup mixture. Bring to a boil. Reduce heat, cover and simmer for approximately 15 minutes.
**Serves 3-5**

# POTATO SOUP

4 potatoes
2 onions (chopped)
3 stalks celery
    (chopped)
1/2 teaspoon salt
2 Tablespoons butter
1 cup milk
1 cup chicken broth
1/2 teaspoon paprika
1/4 teaspoon pepper

Peel and dice potatoes. Add potatoes, onions and celery into heavy pot with enough boiling water to cover the vegetables. Add salt, cover and cook until potatoes are tender. Drain and press through a sieve. Add butter and heat. Add enough milk and broth to reach desired consistency. Add pepper, paprika and additional salt if needed.

**Simmer for 10-15 minutes.**
**Serves 3-5**

# PUMPKIN SOUP

**3 cups pumpkin (chopped)**
**2-1/2 cups water**
**1/2 cup chicken stock**
**1/2 onion**
**2 garlic cloves**
**1-1/2 Tablespoons butter**
**1/4 teaspoon hot sauce**
**1/4 teaspoon pepper**
**1/4 teaspoon allspice**
**3/4 teaspoon sugar**
**1 cup milk**
**1/2 cup cream**
**1/4 teaspoon nutmeg**
**Salt to taste**

Brown onion and garlic in melted butter. Add chopped pumpkin, water, chicken stock, hot sauce, pepper, allspice and sugar. Cover and bring to boil. Reduce heat and simmer for 30-40 minutes or until pumpkin is tender. Remove from heat and beat until smooth and creamy. Add milk and cream to desired consistency. Heat until thoroughly warmed. Sprinkle with nutmeg and serve.

**Serves 4**

# TOMATO AND RICE SOUP

1 pound beef stew
1 Tablespoon
    shortening
2 cups water
2 cups stewed tomatoes
1-1/2 teaspoons pepper
1/2 teaspoon salt
3/4 cup rice(uncooked)

Brown beef in 1 Tablespoon shortening. Remove excess fat from beef and add water, tomatoes, pepper, and salt. Bring to a brisk boil. Add rice and allow to boil a second time. Cover and reduce heat.
**Simmer — 40 minutes.**
**Serves 4**

# CREAM OF TOMATO SOUP

3 cups tomatoes
1/2 cup celery
    (chopped)
1/4 cup onion
    (chopped)
1-1/2 cups water
3 teaspoons sugar
5 Tablespoons butter
    (melted)
4 Tablespoons flour
4 cups milk
1 teaspoons salt
1/4 teaspoon paprika

Mix tomatoes, celery, onion, sugar and water in saucepan. Simmer for 15 minutes. In separate pan, melt butter and stir in flour. Add milk to flour mixture. Strain liquid from vegetables and add to milk mixture. Add salt and paprika. Serve hot.
**Serves 4-6**

# TURKEY SOUP

**Turkey leftovers**
**1/4 cup water**
**2 cups turnips**
**(diced)**
**2 cups celery**
**(chopped)**
**1 cup onion**
**(chopped)**
**2 cups tomatoes**
**(stewed)**
**2 cups potatoes**
**(diced)**
**1 teaspoon salt**
**1 teaspoon pepper**

Debone leftover turkey and cut into small pieces. Pour water into a heavy pot. Add all ingredients. Cover and simmer for 1-1/2 hours. May be cooked longer. Add additional water if needed.
**Serves 6-8**

*"Home Remedy"*
*— To cure a cold, drink juice from an onion that has been roasted in the ashes of wood from a live oak tree.*

# VEGETABLE SOUP

**1-1/2 pounds ham
  hocks**

**8 cups water**

**1 teaspoon salt**

**1/2 teaspoon pepper**

**2 Tablespoons bacon
  drippings**

**1/4 cup onion
  (chopped)**

**1/2 cup celery
  (chopped)**

**4 pods sweet pepper
  (chopped)**

**2 pods hot pepper
  (chopped)**

**1-1/2 cups corn**

**1-1/2 cups lima beans**

**1-1/2 cups field peas**

**2 cups tomatoes
  (stewed)**

**1/2 cup tomato sauce**

**6 pods okra
  (chopped)**

**3 medium potatoes
  (diced)**

**1 cup beef stock**

Bring 8 cups water to boil in a large soup pot. Add ham hocks, salt and pepper. Boil until tender (approximately 40 minutes). Using a small skillet, add bacon drippings and brown onion, celery and peppers. Add to ham hocks. When meat begins to separate from bone, add corn, beans, peas, tomatoes and tomato sauce. Cook until corn is tender. Stir occasionally to prevent sticking. Add okra, potatoes and beef stock.

**Simmer 20 minutes or until all vegetables are tender.**
**Serves 6-8**

# CABBAGE SLAW

**1 head cabbage (shredded)**
**1 green pepper (chopped)**
**1 onion (chopped)**
**2/3 cup cooking oil**
**1-1/4 cups vinegar**
**1 cup sugar**

Mix all vegetables. Bring oil and vinegar to a brisk boil and add 1 cup sugar. Bring to a second boil and remove from heat. Pour over cabbage mixture.

**Serves 4-6**

*"Home Remedy"*
*— Give a grouchy person tea made from the root of a wild lilac.*

# CARROT SLAW

**1 cup apple (diced)**
**1 cup raisins**
**1 cup carrots**
**(shredded)**
**1/2 cabbage (shredded)**
**pinch of salt**
**1 Tablespoon**
**mayonnaise**
**1 teaspoon lemon juice**
**1/2 cup nuts**

Mix apples, raisins, carrots, cabbage and salt. Mix lightly with mayonnaise. Sprinkle with nuts and lemon juice. Serve on crisp lettuce leaves.

**Serves 4**

# PICKLED SLAW

1 head cabbage
  (shredded)
3 tomatoes (chopped)
1 onion (chopped)
5 cucumbers (chopped)
10 radishes (chopped)
4 stalks celery
  (finely chopped)
3 carrots (shredded)
1 cup sugar
4 teaspoons salt
1/4 teaspoon turmeric
1/4 teaspoon dry
  mustard
1/4 teaspoon ginger
1/4 teaspoon celery
  seeds
1/4 teaspoon cloves
  (ground)
1/4 teaspoon cinnamon
3/4 cup catsup
1 cup cider vinegar
1/2 cup water

Combine all ingredients except vegetables in a saucepan and bring to a boil. Stir until spices are dissolved. Chill the mixture. Pour over vegetable mixture and toss.

**Makes 8 pints**

# POOR MAN'S CAVIAR

*(eggplant salad)*

**1 eggplant**
**2 onions (chopped)**
**2 cloves**
**2 cloves garlic**
    **(minced)**
**2 tomatoes (chopped)**
**salt to taste**
**1/4 teaspoon red**
    **pepper**
**1 Tablespoon olive oil**
**4 Tablespoons vinegar**

Broil eggplant for 15-20 minutes. Turn to assure even cooking. A cake tester may be used to tell when eggplant is soft all the way through. Remove skin and mash eggplant. Mix with onion, cloves and garlic. Add tomatoes, salt, pepper, vinegar and oil. Serve on bed of greens.

**Serves 4**

*May also be used as a spread for canapes.*

# TOMATO SALAD

**4 cups tomatoes
    (stewed)**

**1/3 cup onion
    (chopped)**

**1/3 cup green pepper
    (chopped)**

**3/4 cup celery
    (chopped)**

**4 Tablespoons sugar**

**6 Tablespoons vinegar**

**2 Tablespoons olive oil**

**2 teaspoons mustard
    seeds**

**1 teaspoon salt**

**1/4 teaspoon pepper**

Drain tomatoes and cut into small pieces. Add onion, green pepper and celery. In a separate container mix remaining ingredients. Add to vegetables. Chill for 6 hours before serving.

**Serves 4-6**

# WILTED SALAD AND RED EYE GRAVY

**1 bunch leaf lettuce**
**1 bunch mustard**
   **greens**
**6 green onions**
**1/2 cup white vinegar**
**4 ham steaks**
**2 Tablespoons**
   **shortening**
**1 teaspoon sugar**
**1/4 cup water**
**1-1/2 teaspoons salt**

Chop lettuce, mustard greens and onions. Put in bowl and toss. Cover and refrigerate until ready to serve. Heat shortening in heavy skillet. Add ham steaks and brown lightly on both sides. Remove the ham and pour drippings into gravy bowl for later use. Heat remaining meat residue left in skillet with 1 teaspoon sugar until browned. Add water and boil for 1/2 minute. Pour into gravy bowl with meat drippings (red eye gravy). Top salad servings with 2 Tablespoons vinegar and 2 Tablespoons gravy. Salt to taste.

*Serve with ham steaks and 'homemade' biscuits. Olive oil may be substituted for red eye gravy.*

**Serves 4**

*"Home Remedy"*
*— Poke roots were used to make poultices to use on cuts and scratches.*

# CHICKEN SALAD

5 tomatoes
1/2 cup cucumber
   (diced)
1-1/2 cups chicken
   (cooked)
1/4 cup nuts
2 Tablespoons
   mayonnaise
salt and pepper to taste

Scald, peel and chill tomatoes. Scoop out tomato pulp. Keep tomato shell to be stuffed. Just before serving mix chicken, cucumber, tomato pulp and nuts with mayonnaise. Season to taste. Fill tomato shells with chicken mixture. Serve on bed of lettuce or other leafy green vegetable.
**Serves 5**

*"Home Remedy"*
*— Eating raw garlic cloves was good for heart trouble.*

# HAM SALAD

**4 cups ham (cooked)**

**3 eggs (boiled)**

**1/4 cup sweet pickles (chopped)**

**1 Tablespoon carrots (grated)**

**1 cup celery (chopped)**

**1 teaspoon mustard**

**1 Tablespoon mayonnaise**

**salt to taste**

**1/4 teaspoon pepper**

**1 teaspoon lemon juice**

Cut ham into small cubes. Add finely chopped eggs, celery, pickles and carrots. Season with salt and pepper (amount of salt will vary according to kind of ham used). Lightly mix in mayonnaise and mustard. Sprinkle lemon juice over the salad. Serve on green vegetable leaves.

**Serves 6**

*A dressing may be served over the salad.*

# TUNA FISH SALAD

**1 cup tuna fish
    (shredded)**

**1/3 cup cabbage
    (shredded)**

**1 cup nuts
    (chopped)**

**3 eggs (boiled)**

**1/3 cup sweet pickle
    (chopped)**

**1/3 cup celery
    (finely chopped)**

**2 Tablespoons
    mayonnaise**

**1 teaspoon mustard**

**1/4 teaspoon salt**

**1/4 teaspoon pepper**

**1/4 teaspoon paprika**

Mix tuna, nuts, eggs, pickles, celery and cabbage. Add salt and pepper. Fold in mayonnaise and mustard. Sprinkle with paprika. Serve on bed of green lettuce leaves.

**Serves 4**

*"Home Remedy"*
*— Tea made from boiled sassafras root was used to build blood.*

# APPLE COCONUT SALAD

**1 cup apple (diced)**
**1 cup celery (diced)**
**3/4 cup coconut (grated)**
**2 Tablespoons lemon juice**
**7 Tablespoons orange juice and pulp**
**3 Tablespoons olive oil**
**1/4 teaspoon salt**
**1/4 teaspoon paprika**
**3 Tablespoons plum jelly**

Combine apple, celery and coconut. Sprinkle with lemon juice. Mix oil, orange juice, salt and paprika in a separate container. Fold in apple mixture. Dot with plum jelly after arranged on bed of lettuce.

**Serves 3**

# BLACKBERRY DELIGHT

1 cup blackberries
1 cup cantaloupe
   (cubed)
1 cup honeydew
   (cubed)
1 cup watermelon
   (cubed)
1 cup grapes
   (seedless)
3 bananas (sliced)
1 Tablespoon powdered
   sugar

Mix all fruit in bowl. Chill for 2 hours. Sprinkle sugar over fruit before serving.

**Serves 5**

# FRUIT SALAD

1 large apple
  (diced)
2 cups grapes
  (seedless)
2 tangerines
  (diced)
1 orange (diced)
1/2 cup raisins
2 bananas (sliced)
1 cup candied cherries
  (chopped)
3/4 cup coconut
  (grated)
1 cup strawberries
  (diced)
2 Tablespoons sugar
1 cup walnuts
  (chopped)
1/2 cup pecans
  (chopped)

Combine all fruits. Add coconut and nuts. Sprinkle with sugar. Chill two hours before serving.

**Serves 6**

# BUTTERMILK SALAD DRESSING

1 Tablespoon
   cornstarch
1 Tablespoon dry
   mustard
1 cup buttermilk
2 eggs (beaten)
1/2 cup white vinegar
1/4 cup lemon juice
1/4 teaspoon salt
1/4 teaspoon pepper
2 teaspoons sugar

Combine cornstarch, dry mustard, salt and pepper. Add in eggs and buttermilk, stirring constantly. Do not boil. Combine vinegar, lemon juice and sugar in a separate bowl. Gradually add this mixture to hot buttermilk. Beat well after every addition. Chill before serving.
**Makes 2-1/4 cups**

# SALAD DRESSING

1/2 cup sugar
1-1/2 teaspoons
   paprika
1-1/2 teaspoons salt
1 teaspoon dry mustard
1/2 cup vinegar
1-1/4 cups olive oil

Combine sugar, paprika, salt and dry mustard. Slowly stir in vinegar and olive oil. Beat the dressing until thoroughly mixed, approximately 3-5 minutes.
**Makes 2 cups**

*"Home Remedy"*
*— Rub a mixture of buttermilk and salt water on a rash or poison ivy to stop the itching.*

# COUNTRY GRAVIES

**Brown Flour Gravy** - Heat 2 Tablespoons fat in skillet. Add 3 Tablespoons flour, 1/4 teaspoon salt and 1/8 teaspoon pepper. Stir until mixture is dark brown. Add 1-1/2 cups cold water. Simmer approximately 5 minutes.

**Cream Gravy** - Melt 2 Tablespoons butter in a heavy skillet. Stir in 2 Tablespoons flour until well blended. Add 1 cup milk. Season to taste. Simmer for approximately 5 minutes.

**Giblet Gravy** - Boil giblets in 3 cups water and set aside. Pour off fat from pan in which poultry has been roasted. Save at least 4 Tablespoons of fat. Add 3 Tablespoons flour and stir until brown. Add 3 cups stock from boiled giblets. Stir until smooth and thickened. Add chopped giblets. Season with salt and pepper. Simmer 5 minutes.

**Red Eye Gravy** - Red eye gravy can only be made with fat left after meat has been fried. Meat must be fried without flour or batter. Pour hot drippings from skillet into gravy bowl. Brown 1 teaspoon sugar in skillet with residue left from fried meat. While very hot add 1/4 cup cold water and simmer 1/2 minute or until residue has blended with water. Put gravy spoon in bowl containing fat before pouring mixture from skillet into bowl. The spoon will help absorb the heat from the hot fat and help prevent splattering.

**Tomato Gravy** - Heat 2 Tablespoons meat drippings in skillet. Stir in 3 Tablespoons flour, 1/2 teaspoon salt and 1/4 teaspoon pepper. When mixture is dark brown, add mixture of 1/2 cup tomato juice and 1-1/2 cups cold water. Simmer approximately 5 minutes.

**meats**

# FROM THE SMOKEHOUSE

That "other" little house out back, referred to as the smokehouse, was a family treasure. The riches that hung from the rafters would tempt royalty.

Summers were long, hot and in general - miserable. Plowing the fields, hands burning from putting out fertilizer, callouses thickening from pulling a crosscut saw through a thick red oak tree were all preparations for winter existence.

But late evenings provided a change of pace from the day's labor. The slightest movement in the direction of the barn would set off a chorus from the hog pasture that could be heard from farm to farm. It was feeding time.

When Papa had a bushel basket of shucked corn over his shoulder and pigs squealed to high heaven, you knew treats were in store before many months passed.

By early fall, those little pigs, brought home in overall pockets in the spring sure had changed in appearance. Visions of hams, bacon, sausage and shoulders hanging in the smokehouse with the fragrance of hickory smoke were mouth watering.

The first frost and leaves turning to orange and gold meant hog-killing time was near. That old meat box had to be cleaned, a couple sacks of salt set in the corner of the smokehouse and some green hickory cut for smoking.

Preparing the meat required a special skill. On hog-killing day the whole family and even the neighbors were there to help. After all - what are neighbors for?

# GRANDPA SHORTY'S RABBIT STEW

2 medium rabbits

8 cups water

1-1/2 Tablespoons salt

1-1/2 teaspoons pepper

1-1/2 cups cooked corn

2 small onions
    (chopped)

5 small potatoes
    (quartered)

2-1/2 cups tomatoes
    (diced)

1/2 pound salt pork

1-1/4 Tablespoons
    butter

1 Tablespoon flour

Bring water to boil in heavy pot. Add rabbit, salt and pepper. Bring back to boil and add corn, onion, tomatoes and pork. Cover and cook on low heat 1 hour. Add potatoes and cook 45 minutes. Stir occasionally to prevent sticking. Mix flour and butter into paste. Stir into stew.

**Simmer — approximately 20 minutes.**
**Serves 5-6**

---

*Grandpa Shorty Dixon was born in the 1880's on Weeks Island. He worked for over 35 years in the salt mines.*

*Shorty had a true affection for the bayous and swamplands around his home. When not working in the mines, he was usually in pursuit of rabbits, coons or turtles. It was a common sight around the island to see Grandpa Shorty with a burlap sack over his shoulder headed out on a day's hunt. And he seldom brought it home empty.*

*After a hunt, Shorty would sit on the porch with neighbors and family telling hunting stories. One of the most remembered around the island was the one about his brief encounter with a black bear and her cub that robbed him of his sack of turtles.*

# BEEF STEW

**2 pounds beef (cubed)**
**2 teaspoons salt**
**1/2 teaspoon pepper**
**2 cups tomatoes**
**  (cooked)**
**2 cups water**
**5 potatoes (quartered)**
**2 onions (quartered)**
**1 cup green beans**
**1/2 cup carrots**

Brown beef cubes. Add salt, pepper, tomatoes, and water. Mix thoroughly and cover. Cook over medium heat 3-5 minutes. Reduce heat and simmer approximately 1 hour. Add potatoes, onions, beans and carrots. Cover and cook 25 minutes or until vegetables are tender. Remove vegetables and meat and thicken with flour to desired consistency. Return all ingredients and simmer five minutes.

**Serves 5-7**

*"Signs of Nature"*
*— Forecasting weather by animal and insect behavior, as well as other patterns and cycles of nature, has long been a practice used by hunters, fishermen and farmers.*

# MEAT BALLS AND RICE

2 pounds beef
(ground)

2 eggs

1/2 onion (chopped)

3 Tablespoons parsley
(minced)

1-1/2 teaspoons salt

1/2 teaspoon pepper

1/8 teaspoon red
pepper

3-1/2 cups tomatoes
and juice (cooked)

1/2 cup water

Mix thoroughly beef, eggs, onion, parsley, 1 teaspoon salt and pepper. Make 15 small meat balls. Combine tomatoes and juice, 1/2 teaspoon salt and water in a large skillet. Bring mixture to boil. Add meatballs. Cover and simmer 30-40 minutes. Remove meat balls from liquid. To thicken liquid for gravy, mix 1 Tablespoon flour to 3/4 cup water and pour into tomato mixture. Add meatballs and simmer 10 minutes.
**Serve over rice.**

# POT ROAST

**2-1/2 pounds beef
     (roast)**
**2 Tablespoons fat**
**1 cup water**
**3/4 cup black coffee**
**1 cup tomatoes
     (chopped)**
**1 onion (sliced)**
**5 carrots**
**2 cups potatoes**
**salt and pepper to taste**

Brown meat on all sides in hot fat. Pour water and coffee over roast. Add salt and pepper. Bring to a brisk boil. Reduce heat and simmer 40 minutes. Add tomatoes, onion and carrots. Simmer 20 minutes. Add potatoes and simmer until vegetables are tender.
**Serves 5-7**

*"Signs of Nature"*
*— If lost in woods, remember, moss grows on the north side of a tree.*

# ROUND STEAK DISH

**3-1/2 pounds round steak**

**1/4 teaspoon pepper**

**1/4 teaspoon salt**

**1/4 teaspoon red pepper**

**6 slices bacon**

**1/3 cup butter**

**1-1/2 Tablespoons brown sugar**

**3 cups tomatoes (cooked)**

**1-1/4 cups water**

Cut small pockets lengthwise in steak. Fill with bacon. Rub steak with seasoning. Heat butter in skillet and brown meat on both sides. Add brown sugar, tomatoes and water. Cover and simmer for 1-1/2 hours or until meat is tender.

**Serves 5-7**

# SKILLET MEAT LOAF

2 pounds ground beef
1/2 cup bread crumbs
6 Tablespoons onion
    (chopped)
2 eggs
1 cup tomato sauce
1 teaspoon salt
1/2 teaspoon pepper
1 Tablespoon butter
1/3 cup water
2 teaspoons mustard
2 Tablespoons
    Worcestershire
    sauce

Combine all ingredients except butter, water, mustard, 1/2 cup tomato sauce and Worcestershire sauce. Mix well. Shape into two meat loaves. Melt butter in a skillet and brown meat loaves on both sides. Cover and cook for 25-30 minutes over low heat. Mix mustard, 1/2 cup tomato sauce, water and Worcestershire sauce. Pour over meat loaf. Simmer uncovered 10-15 minutes.
**Serves 4-6**

# LIVER AND ONION

**2 pounds veal liver**
**salt and pepper to taste**
**1 onion**
**1/2 cup flour**
**1/2 cup water**

Cut liver into 3 inch squares. Season with salt and pepper. Roll in flour and pan fry in shortening. Fry until golden brown on both sides. Turn only one time. Remove liver from skillet and fry onion in drippings, stirring constantly. Return liver to skillet and add water. Cover with tight fitting lid and cook for approximately 5 minutes. Liver will become tough if cooked too long.
**Serves 5**

# LIVER AND RICE

**1 pound pork liver**
**1/4 cup fat**
**1/2 cup onion**
    **(chopped)**
**1/2 cup green pepper**
    **(chopped)**
**1/2 cup celery**
    **(chopped)**
**2 cups rice (cooked)**
**1 cup tomato juice**
**1 teaspoon salt**
**1/2 teaspoon pepper**

Cover liver in boiling water. Simmer 10-12 minutes. Drain and cut into small cubes. Brown liver, onion, pepper and celery in hot fat. Mix rice and tomato juice with liver and vegetables. Add salt and pepper.
**Cover and bake at 350 degrees — 1-1/2 hours.**
**Serves 5-6**

# BARBECUE RIBS

**8 pounds ribs**
**3 Tablespoons lemon juice**
**1/2 teaspoon pepper**
**1/2 teaspoon salt**
**1/2 cup cooking oil**
**4 cups tomato sauce**
**3/4 cup Worcestershire sauce**
**1/4 teaspoon garlic powder**
**1 cup butter**
**1/2 cup brown sugar**
**2 Tablespoons vinegar**
**2 Tablespoons lemon juice**
**1/4 teaspoon red pepper**

Sprinkle 3 Tablespoons lemon juice and pepper over ribs. Allow to set for 1 hour. Rub ribs with oil before putting on fire. Sear meat on both sides. Mix remainder of ingredients in a saucepan and simmer for 20 minutes. Baste ribs with sauce while cooking. Cook until meat begins to separate from bone.
**Serves 6-8**

# BAKED SPARERIBS

**5 pounds spareribs**
**salt and pepper to taste**
**1/8 teaspoon celery salt**
**3 cups bread crumbs**
**1/3 cup butter**
**3 apples (unpeeled and cubed)**
**1/3 cup water**

Cut spareribs into two pieces. Season with salt, pepper and celery salt. Combine bread crumbs, apples, butter and water and toss lightly. Put one-half of ribs with meat side down and top with half of dressing. Add the other half of ribs and top with remaining dressing. **Bake 350 degrees — 1 hour.**

*"Signs of Nature"*
*— Only six weeks until frost when goldenrods bloom.*

# CHARBROILED PORK LOIN

**5-6 pounds pork loin**
**1 cup butter**
**1/4 cup olive oil**
**1 Tablespoon onion powder**
**3/4 Tablespoon garlic salt**
**1-1/2 teaspoons celery seed**
**1 teaspoon pepper**
**1/2 teaspoon salt**
**1/4 cup lemon juice**
**2 Tablespoons brown sugar**
**1 Tablespoon mustard**
**1-1/2 cups Worcestershire sauce**

Make cross cuts to the bone every 2 inches on loin. Mix 1 teaspoon pepper and 1/2 teaspoon salt. Rub into cut sections. Heat olive oil in sauce pan. Add butter and mustard, stirring until mixed. Add balance of ingredients to butter mixture. Place loin over charcoal fire. Lace coals with sassafras chips. Baste as needed with sauce mixture to keep loin moist. Cook until meat separates from bone along edges.
**Serves 4-6**

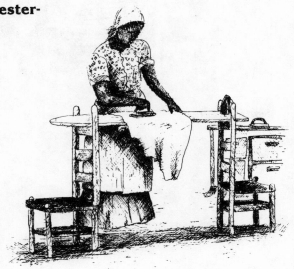

# FRIED PORK CHOPS

**6 pork chops**
**1 cup milk**
**2 eggs**
**1 cup bread crumbs**
**1 Tablespoon flour**
**1/2 cup water**
**1/2 green pepper**
**(chopped)**
**1/2 onion (chopped)**
**1 cup stewed tomatoes**
**and juice**
**salt and pepper to taste**

Rub pork chops with salt and pepper and allow to set for 10 minutes. Beat eggs and milk. Dip seasoned pork chops in milk mixture and roll in bread crumbs. Brown slowly in hot grease. Turn only one time. Remove from pan. Pour grease from skillet, leaving approximately 2 Tablespoons. Add 1 Tablespoon flour and stir until light brown. Add water, green pepper, onion, stewed tomatoes with juice. Return chops to pan.

**Cover and simmer — 30-40 minutes.**
**Serves 6**

## HAM HOCKS AND SWEET POTATOES

**4 pounds ham hocks**
**2 teaspoons salt**
**1/2 teaspoon pepper**
**4 sweet potatoes**
    **(quartered)**

Cover ham hocks with water. Add salt and pepper. Cover and simmer until meat begins to separate from bone. Add sweet potatoes and simmer 30-40 minutes or until potatoes are tender.
**Serves 4-6**

## PICKLED PIG'S FEET

**4 pig's feet**
**2-1/2 teaspoons cloves**
**2 bay leaves**
**4 cups vinegar**
**1 Tablespoon salt**
**1 onion**

Cover pig's feet with water. Boil until meat separates from bone. Strain broth where feet have been boiled. Cut meat into cubes. Combine broth, cloves, bay leaves, vinegar, salt and onion. Boil mixture 30 minutes. Put meat from pig's feet into jars. Pour broth mixture over pig's feet. Seal and let set 5 days before using.

# OVEN-BROILED PORK CHOPS

6 pork chops
1/2 cup Worcestershire
   sauce
1/4 cup lemon juice
1/2 teaspoon celery salt
1/2 teaspoon pepper
1/2 teaspoon onion salt
1/2 teaspoon garlic
   powder

Place chops in flat, shallow tin. Mix Worcestershire sauce and lemon juice. Baste both sides of chops thoroughly with sauce mixture. Mix all dry ingredients and sprinkle one-half of mixture over meat. Broil at 400 degrees until tops of chops are lightly browned. Turn meat and sprinkle with remaining dry ingredients. Cook until lightly browned.

**Broil 400 degrees — 20-30 minutes
Serves 6**

*"Signs of Nature"*
*— When smoke hovers close to ground, there will be a weather change.*

*meats*

# SAUSAGE BALLS

**1 pound pork sausage
(ground)**
**1/2 pound beef
(ground)**
**1/4 teaspoon salt**
**1/4 teaspoon pepper**
**2 Tablespoons
shortening**
**3 cups mashed
potatoes**
**3 eggs**
**1/2 cup milk**
**3 cups bread crumbs**

Combine sausage, beef, salt and
pepper. Make into 1 inch balls.
Brown in 2 Tablespoons shortening. Drain and let cool. Beat eggs
and milk together. When sausage
balls have cooled enough to handle, coat with mashed potatoes.
Dip in egg mixture and roll in bread
crumbs. Let set 30 minutes. Deep
fry until golden brown.
**Makes 18-24 balls**

*"Signs of Nature"*
— *When birds and animals are
excessively active throughout the
day, a weather change for the
worse is near.*

# SAUSAGE AND STEWED POTATOES

**1 pound smoked
   sausage**
**4-5 red potatoes**
**2 Tablespoons flour**

Cut sausage into thin slices and fry. Remove from grease and drain. Peel potatoes and cut into 1 inch cubes. Cover with water and boil until tender. Mix flour with 3/4 cup water. Flour mixture should be very thin with no lumps. Pour mixture into boiling potatoes. Stir gently and add sausage.
**Cook over medium low heat — 5-10 minutes.**
**Serves 4-6**

# PORK ROAST

**10-12 pounds pork
roast
2 cloves garlic
(chopped)
2 onions (chopped)
salt and pepper to taste**

Make slits in roast with knife to a depth of approximately 3 inches deep every 5-6 inches. In a small bowl, mix garlic, onion, salt and pepper. Dampen mixture with water. Rub seasoning over roast. Heat small amount of oil in deep heavy iron pot. Brown roast well on all sides. After browning add water and cover. Let cook on high heat for 5 minutes. Reduce heat and let simmer, turn occasionally.

**Bake approximately — 4 hours or until well done.**

*For additional flavor stuff roast and keep in freezer for 3-4 days before baking.*

# FRIED VENISON STEAK

2 pounds venison
   steak
1 cup buttermilk
1/4 cup water
1 teaspoon salt
1/2 teaspoon pepper
1 cup flour

Mix buttermilk and water in bowl. Soak steaks for 1 hour. Remove steaks and drain. Place steaks on meat board. Sprinkle with salt and pepper. Tenderize steaks by hacking both sides. Roll steak in flour thoroughly, coating both sides. Fry in 1/2 inch hot fat until lightly browned. Turn steaks only one time.
**Serves 4**

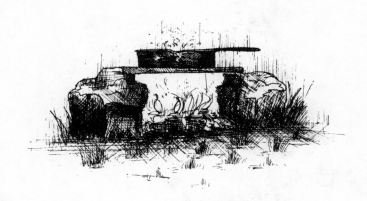

# HUNTER'S MEAT & GRAVY

*(Venison)*

**2-1/2 pounds venison
stew meat**

**3 Tablespoons
shortening**

**2 cups water**

**1 Tablespoon flour**

**1/2 teaspoon salt**

**1/2 teaspoon pepper**

Put venison stew meat in heavy pot with shortening, salt and pepper. Cook until browned. Stir occasionally to prevent sticking. Add 1 cup water. Cover and simmer until tender. Heat 1 cup water to boiling and stir in 1 Tablespoon flour. Add flour mixture to meat. Cover and simmer 15 minutes. Additional water can be added if needed.

**Serves 4-5**

# VENISON SAUSAGE

**7 pounds lean venison**
**3 pounds pork fat**
**1/3 cup salt**
**1/2 cup brown sugar**
**1-1/2 Tablespoons sage**
**2 teaspoons pepper**
**2 teaspoons red**
    **pepper**

Cut venison and fat into 1-2 inch cubes. Mix all ingredients and stir with meats. Run meat through sausage grinder. Make into patties 1/2 inch thick and fry as needed. **Makes 10 pounds sausage.**

*Sausage can be wrapped and frozen for future use.*

*"Signs of Nature"*
*— Stars inside ring around the moon indicate number of days before rain.*

# SMOKED VENISON HAM

**1 venison ham**
**3 white onions**
**6 potatoes**
**4 hot peppers**
**6 sweet peppers**
**4 Tablespoons salt**
**2 Tablespoons pepper**
**3 cloves garlic**
**3 stalks celery**
**   (chopped)**
**1/4 cup lemon juice**
**1/2 cup vinegar**
**1/2 cup olive oil**
**1 cup Worcestershire**
**   sauce**
**1/2 cup butter**

Cover ham with water in large pot. Add all ingredient except Worcestershire sauce and butter. Boil until meat is tender. Remove potatoes, onions and meat. Smoke meat over hickory and sassafras smoke. Melt butter in sauce pan and add Worcestershire sauce. Baste with sauce and turn every 30 minutes while smoking.

**Smoke 2 hours.**

*"Signs of Nature"*
*—When it clouds up on a frost, rain is in the near future.*

**fowl**

## HERE, CHICK, CHICK

Nothing would create havoc as quickly as a bunched-up apron filled with shelled corn and Mama's "here, chick, chick." Seems like her voice always went about two notches higher when she called the chickens, but they recognized that shrill call. Settin' hens left the nest, mother hens left their biddies, roosters quit their quarreling and loose feathers floated in the breeze like new snow. They came from under the house, out of the barn loft and the most peculiar places you could ever imagine.

Mama treasured her chickens and at times treated them almost as if they were part of the family. Some of the older hens even had names. Like all children, we really didn't understand the contribution those chickens made to our day-to-day needs. The Chinaberry switch that was ever present behind the old wood stove sure curtailed the urge to check your marksmanship to see if you could knock that rooster off the woodpile with a green peach or corncob.

Sometimes on birthdays or Christmas we had eggs for breakfast instead of buttered biscuits and syrup. Usually, those eggs were for baking and other cooking. If there were any extras, Mama sold them and that egg money came in mighty handy at times — like when we had to have a new pair of Sunday shoes.

# UNCLE J.V.'S SMOKED GOOSE

1 goose
2/3 cup salt
1 Tablespoon sugar
1 teaspoon saltpeter
1/2 clove garlic

Remove neck, wings and back from goose. Skin neck, leaving skin whole for stuffing. Debone neck, wings and back. Chop into small pieces. Stuff neck skin with chopped meat and tie at both ends. Rub neck, breast and legs with salt. Combine remaining ingredients and rub over all meat. Place meat in crock. Cover with cloth and weight down with plate. Refrigerate for 2 days, turning occasionally. Remove meat and drain. Cover each piece with cheesecloth and smoke for 6-8 hours. Chill and slice.

*Uncle J.V. loves to piddle in the kitchen and experiment with different combinations of foods. When cooking, J.V. always has a batch of candy on the back burner. He has no recipes for any of his candies, but uses whatever there is in the kitchen. Needless to say, this keeps him in high standing with his ten children and all his nieces and nephews.*

*J.V. is active, fun-loving and the life of a party. He also has a bit of "sporting blood." While still a youngster on Weeks Island, he would often put on gloves and go a few rounds with an opponent and has been known to place a bet or two when he could pit a nephew against one of the other boys in a boxing match.*

# BAKED CHICKEN

**1 chicken**
    **3-4 pounds**
**2 teaspoons salt**
**1 teaspoon pepper**
**8 cups bread crumbs**
**1/2 cup butter (melted)**
**1 cup celery**
    **(finely chopped)**
**1/2 onion (sliced)**
**1/2 cup parsley**
**3/4 cup olives**
**1/2 teaspoon sage**
**1-1/2 cups peach**
    **nectar**

Rub 1 teaspoon salt and 1/2 teaspoon pepper over chicken inside and out. Melt butter, add bread crumbs and cook 3-5 minutes. Add celery, onion, parsley, olives, sage, 1 teaspoon salt and 1/2 teaspoon pepper. Stir mixture and cook until vegetables are slightly wilted. Add 1/2 cup peach nectar. Remove from heat and use mixture to stuff hen. Sew up end of chicken. Pour remaining nectar over chicken. Bake uncovered 15 minutes or until chicken is brown. Cover and bake until chicken is tender. Baste as chicken cooks.

**Bake 350 degrees — 2-1/2 hours.**
**Serves 4**

*Additional water may be added if needed.*

# CHICKEN AND CREAM GRAVY

**1 chicken**
**1 teaspoon salt**
**1 teaspoon pepper**
**1 teaspoon paprika**
**1 egg**
**1/2 cup water**
**1 cup flour**
**1-1/2 cups milk**
**1-1/2 cups chicken
   broth**
**1/2 cup light cream**

Cut chicken into frying pieces. Sprinkle 1/2 teaspoon salt, 1/2 teaspoon pepper and 1/2 teaspoon paprika over chicken. Set aside for one hour. Beat 1 egg and 1/2 cup water. Dip chicken in batter and roll in flour. Set aside 4 Tablespoons flour to be used for gravy. Pan fry until thoroughly cooked. Remove from pan and drain. Pour all but 4 Tablespoons drippings from pan. Blend flour with drippings and stir until browned. Add 1/2 teaspoon salt and 1/2 teaspoon pepper. Slowly add 1-1/2 cups milk, 1-1/2 cups chicken broth and 1/2 cup light cream. Add chicken to gravy.

**Simmer — 5-10 minutes.**
**Serves 5-7**

*"Signs of Nature"*
*— When spiders spin webs on a heavy dew, rain is on the way.*

# CHICKEN DISH

1 chicken
    (2-3 pounds)
2 teaspoons salt
1 cup flour
1 teaspoon pepper
1/2 cup bacon fat
4 carrots
4 potatoes
4 onions
1 green pepper
2 cups stewed tomatoes
3 cups water

Cut chicken into quarters. Roll chicken in mixture of flour and 1 teaspoon salt. Melt fat in skillet and brown the chicken. Scrape carrots and potatoes, peel onions and chop pepper. Combine 1 teaspoon salt, pepper, tomatoes and water. Layer vegetables in bottom of heavy pot, add chicken and pour tomato mixture into pot. Cover and bring to a boil, then reduce heat. Cook on medium low 1-1/2 · 2 hours or until chicken is tender.

**Serves 4-6**

# CHICKEN AND DRESSING

1 hen

1 bunch celery
(chopped)

2 green peppers
(quartered)

1 onion (quartered)

2 cups rice (cooked)

4 cups crumbled
cornbread

2 cups cracker crumbs

4 eggs (boiled and
chopped)

1 Tablespoon mustard

3 Tablespoons
mayonnaise

3 Tablespoons pickle
relish

1-1/2 teaspoons salt

2 teaspoons pepper

1 teaspoon sage

### CORNBREAD

1 cup cornmeal
1/2 cup flour
1-1/2 teaspoons baking
powder
1/2 teaspoon salt
1 cup milk

Mix all cornbread ingredients. Heat skillet with 1 Tablespoon fat and sprinkle with meal. Pour mixture into skillet and bake until browned. In large pot cover chicken with water. Add celery, pepper and onion. Boil until chicken is tender. Remove chicken and vegetables from broth. Debone chicken. Mix rice, bread, crackers and eggs with 5-1/2 cups broth. Add mustard, mayonnaise, relish, salt, pepper and sage. Mix well and add chicken. Dressing will have a pouring consistency.

**Bake 400 degrees — 40 minutes**

*Additional broth may be added while cooking if dressing is too dry.*

# CHICKEN AND DUMPLINGS

**1 hen**
**1-1/2 teaspoons pepper**
**1 teaspoon salt**
**3 cups flour**
**1 cup water (chilled)**

Cover hen with water. Add pepper and salt. Boil until meat of chicken is tender. Combine flour and water. Stir until soft dough is formed. Place dough on floured board and knead until firm. Cut off section of dough and roll very thin. Cut into 1-1/2 inch squares. Bring 8 cups broth and chicken to boil. Drop in squares of dough. Continue rolling and dropping dough into broth. Stir lightly when dropping dough squares to prevent dumplings from sticking together. When all dough is in broth, reduce heat and simmer until dough is firm.

**Simmer — 10 minutes.**

*Additional salt and pepper may be added if desired.*

# CHICKEN LIVERS AND GIZZARDS

**1 pound chicken livers**

**1 pound chicken gizzards**

**1 onion (chopped)**

**1/2 green pepper (chopped)**

**1/4 teaspoon garlic salt**

**1/2 teaspoon salt**

**1/2 teaspoon pepper**

**1/2 cup cooking oil**

**1 cup flour**

Season gizzards and livers. Roll in 3/4 cup flour and brown in hot fat. Remove meat and drain. Pour off all but 4 Tablespoons fat. Add 4 Tablespoons flour and stir until brown. Add onions and pepper to roux. Add 2 cups water and stir. Add livers and gizzards.

**Simmer — 10 minutes.**
**Serves 4-6**

# CHICKEN AND CHEESE

**2 cups chicken (cooked)**

**2 cups cheese (grated)**

**3 eggs**

**2 cups milk**

**1/2 teaspoon salt**

**1/2 teaspoon dry mustard**

**1/8 teaspoon paprika**

**1/8 teaspoon pepper**

**6 slices bread**

**3 teaspoons butter**

Remove crust from bread. Butter and cut into 2 inch squares. Arrange the following ingredients in layers in bottom of baking dish: bread on bottom, add 1/2 chicken, cheese, additional layer of bread squares and top with chicken. Beat eggs, milk and seasonings. Pour over layers. Place baking dish in pan containing 1 inch water.

**Bake 325 degrees — 45 minutes.**

Sprinkle with cheese and bake until cheese is light brown.

**Serves 6-8**

*"Signs of Nature"*
*— When blackberry blooms are heavy, the winter will be severe.*

# CHICKEN LIVER AND BACON

**1/2 pound chicken
    livers**
**1/2 pound bacon**
**2 Tablespoons butter**

Slice chicken livers 1/2 inch thick. Cut bacon into 1 inch pieces. Using a skewer, alternate 6 pieces of bacon with 5 pieces of liver. Melt butter and pour over bacon and liver.

**Bake 425 degrees — until crisp.
Serves 4**

*Serve while hot.*

# CHICKEN LOAF

**2 cups chicken
(cooked)**
**2 cups rice (cooked)**
**2 eggs**
**2/3 cup tomato juice**
**1/2 cup bread crumbs**
**Salt to taste**
**1/4 teaspoon paprika**
**1/2 cup green peppers
(chopped)**
**1/2 cup celery
(chopped)**
**2 Tablespoons onion
(chopped)**
**4 Tablespoons pimento**

Combine all ingredients and mix well. Pour into a baking dish.

**Bake 350 degrees — 40-50 minutes.
Serves 6**

# COUNTRY CHICKEN STEW

1 chicken
    (2-1/2 - 3 pounds)
1/2 cup flour
1 teaspoons salt
1/4 teaspoon pepper
6 Tablespoons butter
6 potatoes (quartered)
6 onions (quartered)
6 carrots (sliced)
2-1/2 cups tomatoes
    (stewed)
3 cups water

Cut chicken into serving size pieces. Roll in salt, pepper and flour. Melt butter in skillet and brown all sides of chicken. Put 1/2 of vegetables in bottom of large skillet. Place chicken on top of vegetables. Add remaining vegetables to top of chicken. Pour tomatoes and water over top. Cover and simmer 1 to 1-1/2 hours.
**Serves 6**

# CREAMY CHICKEN BREAST

4 large chicken
 breasts
4 Tablespoons fat
1 small clove garlic
1 cup chicken broth
1 cup cream
1-1/2 teaspoons salt
1/2 teaspoon pepper
3 teaspoons Worcester-
 shire sauce

Brown breasts in fat. Heat remainder of ingredients in a small
sauce pan until mixture is hot. Pour
sauce over chicken and cover.
**Bake 325 degrees — 1-1/4 hours.
Serves 4**

*"Signs of Nature"*
*— When the katydid starts to sing,
only ninety days until a heavy
frost.*

# EASY CHICKEN CASSEROLE

**1-1/2 cups cooked
    chicken**
**1/2 cup green onions**
**1/2 teaspoon salt**
**1/4 teaspoon pepper**
**2 cups chicken broth**
**1/2 cup rice**
**1/2 cup cheese**

Chop onions and brown in fat. Add salt, pepper and broth and bring to a boil. Add rice. Cover and cook over low heat 20 minutes. Let stand for 15 minutes and add chicken. Heat and sprinkle with cheese.
**Serves 4**

# GRILLED CHICKEN

1 chicken (fryer)

1/4 cup butter

1 cup Worcestershire
   sauce

3 Tablespoons lemon
   juice

1/2 teaspoon garlic salt

1/2 teaspoon onion
   powder

1/2 teaspoon celery salt

1/4 teaspoon pepper

Cut chicken in half. Place on hot grill and sear. Turn and sear other side. Melt butter in pan. Add all ingredients and stir until mixture boils. Baste chicken halves and turn. Continue basting and turning every 5-10 minutes until cooked.

**Grill — approximately 40 minutes.
Serves 4**

# SAVORY CHICKEN

**1 fryer**
    **(2-1/2 pounds)**
**1/4 cup bacon fat**
**1/3 cup green peppers**
    **(chopped)**
**1 onion (chopped)**
**1 clove garlic (minced)**
**2 cups tomatoes**
    **(stewed)**
**1 cup tomato sauce**
**1 teaspoon salt**
**1/2 teaspoon pepper**
**1/4 teaspoon celery**
    **seed**
**2 bay leaves**

Cut fryer into 6-8 pieces. Brown in fat. Remove chicken from fat to drain. Add peppers, onion and garlic. Cook until slightly wilted. Add tomatoes, tomato sauce, salt, pepper, celery seed and bay leaves. Bring to a boil, add chicken, baste and cover.
**Simmer 40-50 minutes**
**Serves 6**

*Serve over rice.*

*"Signs of Nature"*
— *The twelve days after Christmas will indicate the weather for each of the following months.*

# SOUTHERN FRIED CHICKEN

**1 large fryer**
**1 cup cream or milk**
**2 Tablespoons water**
**2 eggs**
**2 cups flour**
**Salt and pepper**
**1/2 teaspoon paprika**
**1 cup bacon fat**
**1 cup shortening**
**1 Tablespoon butter**

Cut chicken into frying pieces. Add salt and pepper to chicken. Set aside for 15 minutes. Mix cream, water, eggs and beat. Pour cream mixture over chicken and allow to soak for one hour. Add paprika to flour, then roll chicken in flour. Melt bacon fat, shortening and butter in skillet. Drop chicken in hot grease and fry on medium heat until golden brown.

**Serves 4-6**

# FRIED DUCK

1 duck
1 cup flour
2 teaspoons salt
1/2 teaspoon pepper
1/4 teaspoon red
    pepper
2 Tablespoons paprika
1/4 cup butter
4 Tablespoons
    shortening
1/4 cup water

Cut duck into serving pieces. Mix flour, salt, pepper and paprika in brown paper bag. Drop 2 or 3 pieces of duck at a time into bag and shake vigorously. Heat butter and shortening in heavy skillet. Fry duck in hot grease until lightly browned, turning only one time. Reduce heat, add water and cover.

**Simmer until duck is tender.
Serves 4-6**

# CREAMED TURKEY

3 Tablespoons butter
4 Tablespoons flour
1-1/2 cups turkey broth
1-1/4 cups milk
1/2 teaspoon salt
1/2 teaspoon paprika
1/8 teaspoon pepper
2 cups turkey (cooked)

Melt butter in a small saucepan. Gradually add flour and stir until blended. Add broth and milk. Stir over low heat until mixture thickens. Add seasoning and turkey.

**Serves 6**

*Serve over rice or noodles.*

# FRIED TURKEY BREAST

**Breast of young turkey**
**Salt and pepper to taste**
**1 cup flour**

Slice turkey cross-grain in 1/4 inch thick slices. Season with salt and pepper. Roll in flour. Deep fry in hot fat until lightly browned.

**Serves 4-6**

*"Signs of Nature"*
— *The weather will be fair if a screech owl hoots.*

# ROAST QUAIL

**8 quail**
**16 slices bacon**
**1/2 cup butter**
**1 lemon (sliced)**
**1/4 teaspoon salt**
**1/4 teaspoon pepper**

Stuff cavity of quail with 1 Tablespoon butter and 1 slice lemon. Rub salt and pepper on outside of quail. Wrap 2 slices of bacon around each bird. Secure bacon with toothpicks. Place birds in a large skillet. Add 1 cup water, cover and bake until tender. Remove cover and broil 10 minutes or until browned.

**Serves 4**

**fish
seafood**

## STUMPIN'

Saturday — spring plowing is finished and the crops are all planted. Normally a work day, but today we're going fishing.

In one corner of the wagon is the old black pot. In another are two gallons of fresh lard, a sack of cornmeal and a box of potatoes. Quilts and kids line the bottom. Spirits are high and even the mule seems to be a bit more frisky than usual.

Mama's old cane pole, warped and crooked from hanging in the barn, is once again to face the task of hauling in the perch — at least enough to 'make the grease stink.' Women and the little fellows roam the banks of the creek, searching out a favorite spot from the last trip. But Papa and some of the older men have bigger plans — 'Old Whiskers' to be exact. Every sunken log and stump is to be explored. Those big catfish love to ease back in a hollow log during the bright of day and just spend a leisure time doing nothing.

Excitement fills the air over a familiar cry, "We got us a big un." Everyone knows 'Old Whiskers' has met his match when one of the men folk reaches up that log and gets a handful of catfish gills.

Nothing is better than 'stumpin' for catfish — except eatin' um on the creek bank.

# SISTER TU TUT'S GARFISH BALLS

Clean and debone garfish. Grind meat (3 cups) and mix with 1 teaspoon salt, 1/4 teaspoon pepper, 1/2 cup chopped onion and 3 Tablespoons parsley (chopped). Make into small balls and roll in flour. Heat 1/2 inch fat in skillet and lightly brown meat balls. Turn to brown all sides. In a separate skillet heat 2 Tablespoons fat. Add 2 Tablespoons flour, stirring until brown. Add 1-1/2 cups cold water. Stir until well blended. Lower heat and add gar balls. Cover and simmer.

**Simmer — 15-20 minutes**

*Serve hot over rice*

---

*Sister Tu Tut is the granddaughter of Grandpa Shorty. Of all the Dixon family, she best carries on the tradition of story-telling. Remembering every detail and making events of yesterday come alive, she relates story after story about her family, neighbors and growing up in Louisiana.*

*Having been the oldest daughter, she learned to cook and manage a household while at the side of her mother, Dula. She also became an accomplished seamstress, learning this art well enough to sew as a means of earning money.*

*Today Tu Tut takes great pride in her role as home-maker and mother of seven.*

# BAYOU CATFISH BITS

**2 pounds catfish filets**
**1 teaspoon hot sauce**
**salt and pepper to taste**
**3 eggs (beaten)**
**1-1/2 cups cornmeal**
**Cooking oil**

Rub fish with hot sauce, salt and pepper. Set aside for 1 hour or more. Cut fish into bite-size pieces and dip into eggs. Roll in cornmeal. Fry quickly in deep fat for 2 or 3 minutes, or until golden brown. Drain.

**Serves 4**

*Serve hot*

*"Signs of Nature"*
*— When the sun shines while raining, it will rain the following day at the same time.*

144

# CATFISH ETOUFFEE

**3 pounds boneless
catfish filets**
**2 cups onions (finely
chopped)**
**1/4 cup celery (finely
chopped)**
**1/4 cup bell pepper
(finely chopped)**
**3/4 cup butter**
**1 teaspoon pepper**
**1 teaspoon red
pepper**
**1 teaspoon salt**

Saute onions, celery and pepper until wilted. Cut fish into four-inch squares or larger. Season with salt and pepper before dropping into pot. Turn gently to avoid breaking fish. Do not stir. Move pan or pot back and forth several times to agitate mixture. Turn heat low and simmer.

**Simmer — 20-25 minutes.**
**Serves 4-5**

*Serve hot over rice.*

# CORNEY LAKE BAKED CRAPPIE

**2 pounds crappie
filets**

**3 Tablespoons butter**

**1 onion (minced)**

**1/2 green pepper
(chopped)**

**1 clove garlic
(minced)**

**1/4 teaspoon garlic salt**

**1/2 teaspoon pepper**

**1 teaspoon salt**

**1/4 cup tomato sauce**

**3 Tablespoons
Worcestershire
sauce**

**2 bay leaves**

**6 slices bacon**

**1 teaspoon hot sauce**

**2 Tablespoons lemon
juice**

Melt butter in skillet and saute onion, green pepper and garlic. Add remaining ingredients, except bacon and lemon juice into mixture. Simmer 10 minutes. Line bottom of baking dish with 3 slices of bacon. Place filets on bacon. Top filets with remaining bacon. Baste with sauce. Cover and bake. Baste occasionally while baking. Sprinkle with lemon juice before serving.

**Bake 325 degrees — 1 hour.
Serves 4**

# CRAB LOAF

3 pounds crab meat

2 teaspoons salt

1-1/2 cups milk

1 onion (finely
  chopped)

2 Tablespoons pimento

2 green onion tops
  (chopped)

3 eggs (beaten)

2-1/2 cups bread
  crumbs

1/2 teaspoon pepper

2 Tablespoons
  Worcestershire
  sauce

1/2 teaspoon celery salt

1/2 teaspoon red
  pepper

8 slices bacon

Combine all ingredients except bacon. Blend thoroughly. Lay 4 slices bacon in bottom of loaf pan. Pack crab mixture into loaf pan. Top with 4 slices of bacon.

**Bake 350 degrees — 50 minutes.**

*Makes 2 loaves*

# CRAYFISH DUNK

Boil 4 pounds crayfish tails in salted water for 15-20 minutes or until tender. Place tails over bowl of chopped ice to chill.

### SAUCE

1/2 cup catsup
1/2 cup chili sauce
1/2 cup horseradish
1-1/2 teaspoons Worcestershire sauce
1/4 teaspoon salt
1/4 teaspoon red pepper
2 teaspoons lemon juice

Mix all ingredients to make a sauce for dipping crayfish.

*"Signs of Nature"*
*Red in the morning — sailors take warning.*
*Red at night — sailors delight.*

# ERKIE'S OYSTER PIE

1 dozen oysters
 (with liquid)

1/4 cup milk

4 Tablespoons fat

4 Tablespoons flour

3 Tablespoons butter

4 Tablespoons green
 onions (chopped)

1 Tablespoon parsley
 (chopped)

1 teaspoon lemon juice

salt and pepper to
 taste

1 teaspoon red hot
 sauce

2 pie crusts

Heat fat in heavy skillet. Stir in flour until browned. Reduce heat and add oysters with liquid and milk. Stir until thickened. Add all remaining ingredients and simmer 5-7 minutes. Pour mixture into pie crust. Cover with second pie crust. Pinch edges of crust to seal. Perforate top crust with fork.

**Bake 350 degrees — 50 minutes.**
**Serves 4**

# FISH N' SHUCKS

3 cups fish
   (cooked)

1/4 cup green onion
   (chopped)

2 Tablespoons green
   pepper (chopped)

4 Tablespoons butter

2 Tablespoons flour

1/2 cup milk

2 Tablespoons celery
   (minced)

2 Tablespoons parsley
   (chopped)

1/2 teaspoon salt

1/4 teaspoon pepper

1/4 teaspoon red
   pepper

3 Tablespoons
   Worcestershire
   sauce

1 teaspoon soy sauce

1 egg (beaten)

Saute onions and pepper in 2 Tablespoons butter. Melt 2 Tablespoons butter. Stir in flour. Add milk and blend thoroughly until smooth and thick. Combine all remaining ingredients, except fish, and add to sauted onions. Add sauce and stir until well mixed. Add fish to mixture. Spoon into corn shucks. Roll and tie ends.

**Bake 375 degrees — 50-60 minutes. Serves 4-5**

*Leftover fried fish may be used.*

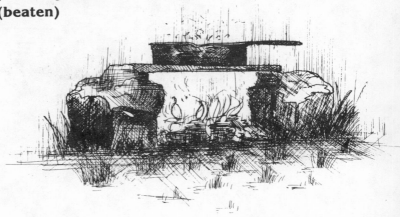

# FRIED FISH

**2-3 pounds fish**
**2-1/2 cups yellow**
**cornmeal**
**1-1/2 Tablespoons salt**
**1/2 teaspoon pepper**
**1 egg**
**1 cup milk**

Cut fish into pan-size pieces. Mix egg and milk in bowl for batter. Dip fish in egg batter and roll in mixture of meal, salt and pepper. Deep fry in hot fat until browned.
**Serves 3-4**

*"Signs of Nature"*
*— When the wind blows from the West, fish bite the best.*

# FRIED FROG LEGS

8 frog legs
3/4 cup lemon juice
1/4 cup water
1 teaspoon salt
1/2 teaspoon pepper
1 cup flour
1 teaspoon baking
   powder
1 Tablespoon sugar
1 egg
1 cup milk

Marinate frog legs in lemon juice, water, 1/2 teaspoon salt and pepper for 1 hour. Mix 1/4 cup flour and all remaining ingredients in separate bowl for batter. Remove frog legs from marinade. Dip in batter, coating thoroughly. Roll in remaining flour. Cover and fry in hot fat until tender. Remove cover and brown lightly.

**Serves 4**

# OVEN BROILED FISH

1 4-5 pound bass (whole)

1 Tablespoon salt

1 teaspoon pepper

6 strips bacon

1 onion (chopped)

1 cup apple (diced)

2 lemons (thinly sliced)

1 green pepper (chopped)

1 teaspoon garlic powder

1 teaspoon celery salt

1/4 cup butter

3/4 cup Worcester-shire sauce

2 Tablespoons soy sauce

Clean fish. (Do not skin.) Remove head and empty cavity. Place 3 strips bacon in bottom of shallow baking tin. Mix onion, apple, lemon and green pepper. Layer 1/3 of mixture on bacon strips. Sprinkle both sides of fish with salt and pepper and place fish on vegetable mixture. Put 1/3 mixture in fish cavity and remaining 1/3 on top of fish. Place 3 strips bacon on top of fish and vegetable bed. Melt butter in saucepan. Add Worcestershire and soy sauce. Add remaining ingredients and bring to boil. Baste fish regularly. Do not turn. Bake until meat separates from bones.

**Bake 375 degrees — approximately 1 hour.**
**Serves 4-5**

*Serve hot*

# OYSTER PUFFS

**1 dozen oysters**
**5 eggs**
**2 Tablespoons butter**
**1/2 teaspoon salt**
**1/4 teaspoon pepper**
**4 Tablespoons heavy
    cream**
**1/4 teaspoon paprika**

Beat eggs and stir in cream, oysters and seasoning. Melt butter in skillet and add oyster mixture. Cook over low heat, stirring occasionally until mixture begins to thicken and becomes fluffy.

**Serves 5-6**

# SALMON PATTIES

**2 cups salmon**
**2 eggs (beaten)**
**1/2 cup onion**
 **(chopped)**
**1 teaspoon pepper**
**1/2 teaspoon red**
 **pepper**
**2 teaspoons salt**
**1 teaspoon**
 **Worcestershire**
 **sauce**
**1 Tablespoon lemon**
 **juice**
**1 cup flour**
**1/2 cup oil**

Drain salmon and mix with eggs, onion, pepper, salt and Worcestershire sauce. Make into 8 small patties. Sprinkle with lemon juice. Roll in flour and fry in oil until brown on both sides, turning only one time.

**Serves 6**

*"Signs of Nature"*
*— When the points of the moon hang down, it will rain within three days.*

# SHRIMP BAKE

**2 cups shrimp
(cooked)**
**3 Tablespoons oil**
**1/2 onion (chopped)**
**3 green onions
(chopped)**
**4 Tablespoons green
pepper (chopped)**
**1 cup tomato sauce**
**1 cup rice (cooked)**
**2 cloves garlic**
**1/4 teaspoon salt**
**1/4 teaspoon pepper**
**1/4 teaspoon red
pepper**

Saute chopped vegetables in oil.
Add tomato sauce and simmer 20-
30 minutes. Add shrimp, rice and
seasoning. Pour into shallow baking dish.

**Bake 375 degrees — 10-12 minutes.
Serves 4**

# SHRIMP AND GRAVY

**1 pound shrimp**
**1 cup bread crumbs**
**2 eggs**
**1/2 onion (chopped)**
**3 cloves garlic**
    **(minced)**
**2 Tablespoons**
    **Worcestershire**
    **sauce**
**4 Tablespoons green**
    **onions (chopped)**
**Salt and pepper to**
    **taste**
**3 Tablespoons flour**

## GRAVY

**3 Tablespoons flour**
**4 Tablespoons oil**
**1/2 onion (chopped)**
**1 green pepper**
    **(chopped)**
**1 cup tomato sauce**
**1/2 teaspoon sugar**
**Salt and pepper**
**3 cups water**

Grind shrimp, onion and garlic. Add remaining ingredients and mix thoroughly. Shape into small balls and roll in flour.

### Gravy

Make a roux with flour and oil. Saute' onions and green pepper in roux. Add water and stir until mixture is smooth. Combine remaining ingredients and stir until well blended. Add shrimp balls and simmer.

**Simmer 2 hours.**
**Makes 12-15 balls**

*Additional water may be added if needed.*

# TUNA CASSEROLE

1 can tuna (7 oz.)
1/2 teaspoon salt
1/4 teaspoon pepper
1/2 teaspoon paprika
2 teaspoons lemon
    juice
1 cup bread crumbs
3/4 cup milk
3 eggs (separated)

Mix flaked tuna, salt, pepper, paprika and lemon juice. Simmer bread crumbs in milk for 5 minutes. Add fish mixture to egg yolks and mix well. Fold in stiffly beaten egg whites. Pour into baking dish. Set dish in pan of water and bake.

**Bake 350 degrees — 40-50 minutes.
Serves 4-6**

*"Signs of Nature"*
*— When the wind blows from the East, fish bite the least.*

**sweets**

## GATHERING UP

Folks haven't always been the way they are today. We used to know our neighbors and even the neighbors' kin. Visitors were always special. When we saw somebody headed up that dusty road toward our house, we knew he had to be coming to see us. No one else lived for a mile or more in any direction.

Sometimes on Saturday just before dusk, there would be a wagonload of neighbors coming down that road —maybe even two. You could bet things were "fixing" to get lively. After all the handshaking, hugging and kid kissing, Mama would head for the kitchen safe. With a little sugar, flour, eggs and that ever present ingenuity, she'd cook up some choice goodies for a country gathering.

Just before dark someone would break out a rusty old 'juice' harp or harmonica and that was the cue for Papa to go to the 'chiff-robe' and unwrap that old banjo. It was more glue and cracks than wood, but the melodies were loud and true. Singing and dancing could last until sunrise — but not much later, because Sunday was church day and a day of rest.

# MADEA'S BREAD PUDDING

**4 eggs**
**2 cups sugar**
**1 teaspoon salt**
**1 teaspoon nutmeg**
**1 teaspoon cinnamon**
**4 cups toasted bread crumbs (rolled)**
**1 cup butter**
**1 quart milk**
**2 Tablespoons baking powder**
**1 teaspoon vanilla**

Toast bread, roll it, put the pieces left back in the oven and repeat until you have 4 cups. Blend butter and sugar together. Add eggs, bread crumbs, milk and other ingredients.

**Bake 350 degrees — until pudding becomes firm.**

### Sauce

In a small saucepan, mix 1 pint milk, 1 Tablespoon cornstarch, 2 eggs and 1 cup sugar stir until mixture thickens. Add vanilla flavor.

*Raisins and fruit may be added to pudding.*

---

*Ethel Johnson is the youngest daughter of Julia Pettaway. She is one of the two surviving children from Big Mama's family of nine. Madea, as she is affectionately called by her niece, Ethel Dixon, is by any standard an expert at cooking in that old black pot.*

*A few years ago she was invited to a relative's home for Easter. She arrived with the entire "Easter Dinner" neatly packed in the back seat and trunk of her car — roast duck, baked sweet potatoes, rolls, two vegetables, two pies, two cakes and bread pudding.*

# APPLESAUCE CAKE

2 cups flour
1 cup sugar
2 eggs
1-1/2 cups applesauce
1 teaspoon soda
1 teaspoon salt
1 cup raisins
1 cup dates
1 cup pecans
   (chopped)
2 Tablespoons
   blackberry jam
1 teaspoon cinnamon
1/2 teaspoon nutmeg
1/2 cup shortening
1 teaspoon vanilla

Sift flour, cinnamon, nutmeg and salt. In a separate bowl cream sugar and shortening thoroughly. Add eggs. Stir soda into applesauce. Combine flour mixture and remaining ingredients. Pour into tube pan.

**Bake 350 degrees — 1 hour.**

# APPLE CAKE

4 apples (firm)
3 teaspoons cinnamon
2-1/2 cups sugar
3 cups flour
3 teaspoons baking
   powder
1/2 teaspoon salt
1 cup cooking oil
4 eggs
1/2 cup orange juice
3 teaspoons vanilla

Peel and slice apples, sprinkle with cinnamon and 1/4 cup sugar. Cover and set aside. Sift flour and baking powder, salt, sugar. Add cooking oil, eggs, juice and vanilla. Make a layer of apples then pour batter. Alternately layer apples and batter. The top layer of cake should be made from apples.

**Bake 350 degrees — 1-1/2 to 2 hours.**

# BUTTERMILK CAKE

**1 cup buttermilk**
**1 cup shortening**
**2-1/2 cups sugar**
**1 teaspoon salt**
**3 cups flour**
**4 eggs**
**1/2 teaspoon soda**
**1 Tablespoon hot water**
**1 teaspoon vanilla**

Cream shortening and sugar. Add 1 egg at a time and beat well after adding each. Add sifted flour and salt alternately with the buttermilk. Blend well. Stir in soda dissolved in the hot water and 1 teaspoon vanilla. Pour into tube pan.

**Bake 350 degrees — 45 minutes.**
**Reduce heat and bake 325 degrees — 20 minutes.**

# THE CHRISTMAS CAKE

2-1/2 cups cake flour
2-1/2 teaspoons baking powder
1/4 teaspoon salt
3/4 cup butter
1-1/4 cups sugar
8 egg yolks
3/4 cup milk
1-1/4 teaspoons lemon flavor
1-1/4 teaspoons vanilla flavor

### FROSTING

1/2 cup sugar
1/4 cup corn syrup
2 Tablespoons water
3 egg whites
2 teaspoons vanilla

Sift flour and baking powder twice. Cream butter and sugar until mixture is creamy and light. Add egg yolks that have been beaten until very thick. Add dry ingredients alternately with milk and flavorings. Beat well after each addition. Pour into 2 - 9 inch greased cake pans.

**Bake 375 degrees — 25 minutes.**

### Frosting

Combine sugar, corn syrup and water. Cover and bring to brisk boil. Remove cover and boil until hard ball stage is reached when dropped into cool water. Beat egg whites until stiff peaks form. Gradually pour hot syrup into egg whites, beating while mixing. Add vanilla.

*Miss Bonnie grew up on a farm in rural central Louisiana. — "This recipe is very special. Mama baked this cake the day before Christmas Eve every year for as long as I can remember. The cake could not be touched, except for licking the bowl, until after supper on Christmas Eve."*

165

# CHOCOLATE SHEET CAKE

**1/2 cup buttermilk**
**1/4 teaspoon soda**
**4 Tablespoons cocoa**
**1 cup butter**
**1 cup water**
**2 cups sugar**
**2 cups flour**
**3 eggs**
**2 teaspoons vanilla**

Mix 1/4 teaspoon soda with 1/2 cup buttermilk and set aside for 10 minutes.. Heat cocoa, butter and water in heavy skillet until thoroughly mixed. Sift flour and sugar in mixing bowl and combine with cocoa mixture. Add eggs, buttermilk and vanilla. Mix well. Pour into greased and floured baking pan (15-1/2 x 10-1/2 x 1).
**Bake 400 degrees — 20 minutes.**

### ICING

**4 Tablespoons cocoa**
**1/2 cup butter**
**7 Tablespoons milk**
**2 teaspoons vanilla**
**1 box powdered sugar**
**1-1/2 cups pecans**

### Icing

Heat cocoa, butter and milk in heavy skillet until thoroughly mixed. Sift powdered sugar in mixing bowl and add cocoa mixture. Add vanilla and pecans. Mix well. Spread over hot cake.

*Spread icing over cake while hot.*

# CHOCOLATE SPICE CAKE

4 (1 ounce) squares
   unsweetened
   chocolate
2/3 cup shortening
2 cups flour
2 cups sugar
1 teaspoon baking
   powder
1 teaspoon soda
1 teaspoon salt
1 teaspoon cloves
1 teaspoon cinnamon
1 Tablespoon coffee
   (brewed)
1-1/2 cups buttermilk
3 eggs
2 teaspoons vanilla

### FROSTING
2 eggs (whites)
1/2 cup water
1-1/4 cups sugar
1-1/2 teaspoons corn
   syrup
1 teaspoon vanilla
1 cup walnuts
   (chopped)

Melt chocolate and set aside to cool. Stir shortening to soften. Sift in flour, sugar, baking powder, soda, salt, cloves, cinnamon and coffee. Add 1 cup of buttermilk and beat until flour is thoroughly blended. Stir in 1/2 cup buttermilk, eggs, chocolate and vanilla. Beat until thoroughly mixed. Pour into greased and floured 13 x 9 x 2 baking pan.

**Bake 350 degrees — 40 minutes.**

### Frosting
Place all ingredients except eggs, vanilla and walnuts in a large double boiler. Cook, beating constantly until the mixture forms hard balls when dropped into cool water. Beat egg whites until stiff peaks form. Gradually pour in hot syrup, beating while mixing. Add vanilla. Fold in nuts.

# DO JOHNNY'S SCRATCH CAKE

**2-1/4 cups flour**
**3 teaspoons baking**
**powder**
**1 teaspoon salt**
**1-1/2 cups sugar**
**1/2 cup shortening**
**1 cup milk**
**1 teaspoon vanilla**
**3 eggs**

### ICING

**1/2 cup butter**
**3 Tablespoons cocoa**
**6 Tablespoons cream**
**2 teaspoons vanilla**
**1 box powdered sugar**

Sift all dry ingredients, except sugar. Cream sugar and shortening, stir in milk and flour mixture until well blended. Add vanilla and eggs. Pour into 2 - 9 inch cake pans.
**Bake 350 degrees — 20 to 25 minutes.**

### Icing

Melt butter. Add remaining ingredients and beat until smooth.

# FRUIT CAKE

**4 cups cake flour**
**1 teaspoon mace**
**1 teaspoon nutmeg**
**3 teaspoons cinnamon**
**1/2 teaspoon baking soda**
**3 pounds dates**
**2 pounds raisins (seedless)**
**1 pound citron (sliced)**
**2 cups pecans**
**1 pound butter**
**2 cups light brown sugar**
**10 eggs (separated)**
**1 cup coffee (brewed)**

Sift flour, spices and soda together twice. Mix with fruits and nuts. Cream butter and sugar together until fluffy. Beat yolks until thick and whites until stiff. Add to creamed mixture. Add flour and fruit mixture. Add coffee. Pour into greased pans.
**Bake 300 degrees — 3-4 hours.**

*Traditionally the North and Central areas of Louisiana have long been most influenced by a strong Protestant following. Abstention from alcoholic beverages is still one of the dominating doctrines followed. Even the most staunch followers sometimes take exception at Christmas time. It is considered 'okay' to add 'flavoring' to fruitcakes and eggnog.*

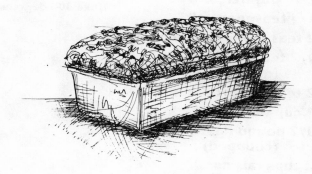

*sweets*

# FIG CUPCAKES

1 cup dried figs
2 cups flour
1 teaspoon salt
2 teaspoons cinnamon
1 teaspoon ginger
1/2 cup shortening
1 cup sugar
3 eggs
1/2 cup milk

Pour boiling water over figs. Cover and let stand 5 minutes. Drain and dry. Sift all dry ingredients.Cream shortening and sugar until fluffy. Add eggs and beat well. Add flour mixture alternately with milk. Fold in chopped figs. Fill muffin tins 2/3 full.

**Bake 400 degrees — 20 minutes.
Makes 12-15**

# FIG LOAF

1 cup shortening
2 cups brown sugar
5 eggs
3 cups cake flour
3 teaspoons baking
    powder
1/4 teaspoon salt
2 teaspoons cinnamon
1/2 teaspoon cloves
    (ground)
2 teaspoons nutmeg
1 cup water
1/2 pound figs
    (chopped)
2 cups raisins

Cream shortening and add sugar. Beat until mixture is fluffy. Beat in eggs. Sift dry ingredients twice and alternately add water and flour mixture. Fold in fruits. Pour in loaf pan.

**Bake 300 degrees — 2 hours.**

170

# GINGER CUPCAKES

**2/3 cup molasses**
**1/2 cup sugar**
**1/2 cup butter**
**1 teaspoon ginger**
**1 teaspoon cinnamon**
**1 teaspoon baking soda**
**2 cups cake flour**
**1 cup sour milk**
**3 eggs (beaten)**

Combine molasses, soda, sugar, butter and spices in saucepan. Bring to a boil. Cool and alternately add flour, eggs and milk. Pour into muffin tins.

**Bake 350 degrees — 15 minutes.**
**Makes 16 cupcakes**

*May be frosted and sprinkled with coconut.*

# HURRY-UP CAKE

2-1/4 cups flour
3 teaspoons baking
    powder
1 teaspoon salt
1-3/4 cups sugar
1/2 cup shortening
1-1/4 cups pecans
    (chopped)
4 eggs
1/2 cup orange juice
3/4 cup milk
1 teaspoon vanilla
3 teaspoons orange
    rind (grated)

Sift all dry ingredients. Add shortening, 3/4 cup nuts, eggs, milk, vanilla, orange juice and rind. Beat until well blended. Pour into 10 inch square pan. Sprinkle with 1/2 cup nuts.
**Bake 350 degrees — 50 - 60 minutes.**

*Uncle Hilton sits on the edge of a chair and chuckles as he talks about growing up and how things have changed. "We seldom had flavoring other than vanilla. When Mama made a cake, she would send me out to pick lemon leaves to line the bottom of the pan to give the cake a lemon flavor."*

# OLD FASHIONED POUND CAKE

**3 cups sugar**
**1 cup shortening**
**6 eggs (separated)**
**2 teaspoons lemon
    extract**
**3 cups sifted flour**
**1/2 teaspoon salt**
**1/4 teaspoon soda**
**1 cup buttermilk**

In large mixing bowl, blend sugar and shortening until light and fluffy. Add egg yolks one at a time, beating well after each. Add lemon extract. Sift dry ingredients together. Add to first mixture alternately with buttermilk. (Begin and end with dry ingredients.) Beat egg whites until stiff, fold carefully into batter. Pour into 10 inch greased and floured tube pan.

**Bake 350 degrees — 1 hour and 10 minutes.**

*Serve with fresh or frozen berries and whipped cream. Frost if desired.*

173

## SUGAR APPLE TREATS

**6 cups apples (sliced)**
**1-2/3 cups sugar**
**1 Tablespoon lemon**
**      juice**
**1/4 cup water**
**2 teaspoons cinnamon**
**1/2 cup flour**
**1/3 cup butter**

Layer apples in bottom of buttered baking dish. Fill pan halfway and sprinkle 1/3 cup sugar over apples. Continue layering apples. Sprinkle 1/3 cup sugar over each layer. Pour lemon juice and water over the top and sprinkle with mixture of cinnamon, flour and remaining sugar.

**Bake 375 degrees — 45 minutes.**

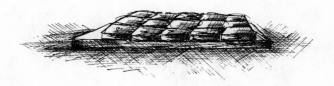

## SUGAR PUFFS

Mix 1 cup self-rising flour with enough milk to make a thin batter. Add 1 egg, 1 Tablespoon of sugar and beat until thoroughly mixed. Drop from a spoon into medium hot grease. The mixture will puff out and turn brown in seconds. Turn immediately and remove from grease. Add 1/2 cup sugar to bag and shake as you drop puffs into sugar.

# CARAMEL CANDY

**2 cups cream**
**1-1/3 cups corn syrup**
**2 cups sugar**
**3/4 cup butter**
**1 teaspoon vanilla**
**1-1/2 cups pecans
  (chopped)**

Mix 1 cup cream, syrup and sugar. Cook over low heat, stirring constantly until mixture boils. Slowly add remainder of cream and butter. Keep candy boiling while adding ingredients. Cook until candy forms a firm ball when dropped into water. Add vanilla to mixture. Put pecans in bottom of buttered 10-inch square pan. Pour mixture over nuts. Let stand 6-8 hours. Cut into squares.

**Makes 2 pounds**

# CHOCOLATE FUDGE

2 cups sugar
1/2 cup butter
3/4 cup evaporated
    milk
2 cups pecans
15 marshmallows
1 teaspoon vanilla
6 ounces chocolate
    pieces

Mix sugar, milk and butter. Bring to a boil quickly, stirring constantly. Cook until mixture forms a hard ball when dropped into cold water. Remove from heat. Add pecans, marshmallows, vanilla and chocolate. Stir only to blend. Drop by teaspoon onto waxed paper. Let cool.

**Makes 24 pieces**

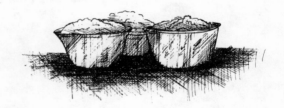

# FOOL-PROOF DIVINITY

**2-3/4 cups sugar**
**2/3 cup white corn**
    **syrup**
**1/2 cup water**
**2 egg whites**
**1 teaspoon vanilla**
**2/3 cup chopped**
    **pecans**

Beat egg whites until stiff peaks are formed. Set aside for later use. Mix sugar, corn syrup and water over low heat, stirring until sugar is dissolved. Cook without stirring until a small amount of mixture forms a hard ball when dropped into very cold water. Remove from heat. Gradually pour syrup mixture into beaten egg whites, stirring constantly. Add vanilla and beat until mixture holds its shape and becomes slightly dull. Fold in nuts. Drop mixture from tip of buttered spoon onto waxed paper.

**Makes 24 pieces**

*Use 1 Tablespoon less water on humid days.*

# HOLIDAY CANDY

1 cup brown sugar

1 cup sugar

3/4 cup water

3 Tablespoons corn
    syrup

2 egg whites
    (stiffly beaten)

1 teaspoon vanilla

1-1/2 cups pecans
    (chopped)

Mix sugar and water in saucepan. Stir over low heat until sugar is dissolved. Add syrup and cook to hard ball stage. Pour mixture over stiffly beaten egg whites. Beat until mixture is light and fluffy and will pile up without spreading. Add vanilla and nuts to mixture. Drop by spoonful onto waxed paper.

**Makes 3 dozen pieces**

# PRALINES

2 cups sugar
1 teaspoon soda
1 cup buttermilk
1/8 teaspoon salt
2 Tablespoons butter
2-1/2 cups pecans

In a heavy saucepan, combine sugar, soda, buttermilk, salt and butter. Cook over high heat for 5 minutes. Stir constantly until candy reaches soft ball stage approximately 5 minutes. Remove from heat and let cool slightly. Add pecans. Beat until light and creamy. Drop from tablespoon onto waxed paper and let cool.

**Makes 15-18**

# PEANUT BRITTLE

**2 cups sugar**
**1 cup corn syrup**
**2 cups raw peanuts**
**2 teaspoons soda**
**2 Tablespoons butter**
**1 teaspoon vanilla**

Cook sugar and corn syrup until sugar is dissolved. Add peanuts and cook until mixture turns a golden color. Add butter, vanilla and soda. Stir lightly and pour onto buttered cookie sheet.

# PEANUT BUTTER TREATS

**1 cup brown sugar**
**1 cup sugar**
**1 cup shortening**
**1 cup peanut butter**
**3 eggs (beaten)**
**2 teaspoons soda**
**1-1/2 cups flour**

Cream shortening and sugar. Add peanut butter and eggs. Sift flour and add all other ingredients. Form 1 inch dough balls. Place on cookie sheet and press with fork.
**Bake 350 degrees — 8 - 10 minutes.**

# TAFFY

2 cups molasses
1 cup sugar
3/4 cup water
1/8 teaspoon soda
4 Tablespoons butter
1 teaspoon vanilla

Cook molasses, sugar and water until mixture reaches a hard ball when dropped into water. Stir as mixture cooks. Remove from heat and add butter, soda and vanilla and stir only enough to mix thoroughly. Pour onto greased pan. When taffy becomes cool enough to handle, pull until it becomes a light color. Stretch into long ropes and cut into small pieces.

# BUTTER COOKIES

**2 cups cake flour**
**3/4 cup butter**
**3/4 cup sugar**
**2 eggs (yolks)**
**1 teaspoon vanilla**

Measure ingredients after they have been sifted. Cream butter and sugar until light and fluffy. Add egg yolks and beat well. Add flour gradually and mix after each addition. Add vanilla and blend. Divide dough in half. Shape into rolls approximately 1-3/4 inches in diameter. Roll in waxed paper and chill overnight. Cut into thin slices.

**Bake 400 degrees — 5-6 minutes or until well done.**
**Makes 5 dozen**

# BUTTERSCOTCH TREATS

**1/4 cup shortening**
**1 cup brown sugar**
   **(packed)**
**2 eggs**
**3/4 cup flour**
   **(self rising)**
**1 teaspoon vanilla**
**1-1/2 cups nuts**

Blend shortening with brown sugar. Stir in eggs, flour, vanilla and nuts. Spread in well-greased 8-inch pan.

**Bake 350 degrees — 20-25 minutes.**
**Makes 16 bars**

# GINGERSNAPS

**1 cup sugar**
**1 cup molasses**
**4 cups flour**
**1 cup butter**
**1 egg**
**1/4 cup water**
**1 teaspoon soda**
**1/2 teaspoon salt**
**1 teaspoon cinnamon**
**1/2 teaspoon ginger**
**1/2 teaspoon nutmeg**

Combine butter, sugar, flour, salt and spices. Add egg, water and molasses. Stir until batter is stiff. Roll out and cut with cookie cutter. Place on ungreased cookie sheet.

**Bake 350 degrees — approximately 10 minutes**
**Makes 36**

*Additional flour may be used if needed.*

# ICEBOX COOKIES

2 cups flour
1-1/2 teaspoons baking
   powder
1/2 teaspoon salt
1/2 cup shortening
1 cup sugar
2 eggs
1 cup coconut
   (shredded)
1 Tablespoon milk
1 teaspoon vanilla

Sift flour, baking powder and salt. Cream shortening and sugar. Add eggs, coconut, milk and vanilla. Mix thoroughly and gradually add flour mixture. Beat well after each addition. Divide dough into two parts and shape into 2 rolls 1-1/2 inches in diameter. Roll in waxed paper. Chill until firm. Cut into 1/4 inch slices.

**Bake 425 degrees — 5 minutes.**
**Makes 7 dozen**

# SOFT MOLASSES COOKIES

1-1/2 cups flour

1-1/2 teaspoons baking powder

1/4 teaspoon soda

1/4 teaspoon salt

1-1/2 teaspoons cinnamon

1/2 teaspoon cloves

1/4 cup shortening

1/4 cup sugar

2 eggs

1/2 cup molasses

1/4 cup buttermilk

1/2 cup raisins

Mix baking powder, soda, salt and spices. Cream in shortening and add sugar. Stir until mixture becomes fluffy. Add beaten eggs and molasses. Add milk and flour alternately, stirring as little as possible. Add raisins. Drop onto lightly greased cookie sheet.

**Bake 400 degrees — 10-12 minutes.**
**Yields 3 dozen**

# SAND TARTS

3 cups flour
1/2 teaspoon salt
2 teaspoons baking
    powder
2/3 cup butter
3/4 cup sugar
2 eggs
1 teaspoon vanilla
1 cup pecans
    (finely chopped)
1/2 cup powdered
    sugar

Sift flour, salt and baking powder. Cream butter, sugar and eggs. Combine the two mixtures and add vanilla. Beat until well blended. Fold in pecans. Chill until dough is firm. Make rolls 1/2 inch in diameter. Cut into 1 inch pieces.

**Bake 275 degrees — until slightly browned.**
**Makes 24**

*Roll in powdered sugar.*

# SUGAR COOKIES

3 cups flour
1 teaspoon soda
1-1/4 cups sugar
1 cup butter
2 eggs
1 teaspoon vanilla

Sift flour and soda. Cream sugar, butter and eggs until light and foamy. Add vanilla and mix thoroughly. Chill dough. Roll into small 1 inch balls and place on greased cookie sheet.

**Bake 375 degrees — approximately 10-12 minutes.**

# TEA CAKES

**3/4 cup shortening**
**2-1/2 cups sugar**
**2 eggs**
**1 cup evaporated milk**
**3-1/2 cups self-rising flour**
**2 teaspoons vanilla**
**1 teaspoon allspice**
**1/4 teaspoon cinnamon**
**1/4 teaspoon nutmeg**

Cream shortening and sugar. Add all remaining ingredients except flour. Mix thoroughly. Add flour (one cup at a time). Roll on a floured board. Dough will be a little hard to work with at first, but it will get firmer as you re-roll. Cut with glass or cookie cutter. Place on ungreased cookie sheet.

**Bake 350 degrees until cookie bottoms begin to turn brown.**
**Makes 24 cookies**

*Additional flour may be added to attain desired dough consistency.*

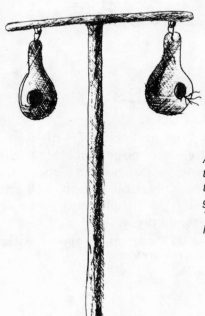

*A grandmother relates — "When I was thirteen, I made tea cakes and sold them to other children for a penny each to buy a gift for my mama on Mother's Day." 'Memaw' still makes these cookies when her grandchildren visit.*

188

# APPLE PIE

1 cup sugar
1/8 teaspoon salt
2 teaspoons cinnamon
1 teaspoon nutmeg
5 cups tart apples
    (peeled & cubed)
1 Tablespoon butter

Mix all dry ingredients and sprinkle half of mixture over pie crust. Add remainder of mixture over apples and dot with butter. Set aside for 20 minutes. Divide pie crust recipe in half. Roll out 1/8 inch thick and moisten bottom half of pie crust. Add apple mixture to pan. Roll remainder of pie crust out 1/8-inch thick and make a top crust. Make several slits in top crust.

**Bake 400 degrees — 1 hour.**

## PIE CRUST

3 cups flour
1 teaspoon salt
1-1/4 cups shortening
6 Tablespoons ice water
1 Tablespoon vinegar
1 egg

### Pie Crust

Cream flour, salt and shortening. Mix egg, vinegar and water. Add to first mixture. Chill before rolling.

# BUTTER ROLL PIE

2 cups flour
3 teaspoons baking
　　powder
pinch of salt
3/4 cup water
1-1/2 cups sugar
3 cups milk
1 teaspoon vanilla
2 teaspoons cinnamon
1/2 cup butter
　　(softened)

Mix flour, baking powder, water and salt. Roll dough out on floured board to 1/4 inch thickness. Dot top of dough with butter. Mix sugar and cinnamon. Sprinkle dough with 6 Tablespoons sugar mixture. Lift edge of dough and roll into 2 inch diameter (roll up like jelly roll). Coat bottom of baking dish with butter. Cut rolled dough into 3 inch lengths (will look like a cinnamon roll) and place in baking dish. Blend milk, vanilla and 4 Tablespoons sugar and cinnamon mixture and bring to a brisk boil. Sprinkle remaining sugar mixture over top. Dot with remaining butter. Pour boiling milk mixture over dough. The rolled dough will rise to top.

**Bake 350 degrees — 30-40 minutes.**
**Serves 4-5**
*Serve hot.*

*Aunt Bessie lived all of her ninety-eight years within one mile of where she was born. In her ninety-third year, she planted and harvested five acres of corn and milked four cows daily. One of the favorite desserts of her family was butter roll pie. She would bake this treat and draw cool water from the well and carry to the field where Poppa and the kids were working.*

# BLACKBERRY COBBLER

**4 cups blackberries**
**1 cup flour**
**1/8 teaspoon salt**
**1/4 cup milk**
**3/4 cup sugar**
**1 Tablespoon butter**
**1 teaspoon baking**
**powder**

Sift all dry ingredients, except sugar. Blend in butter and add milk. Turn onto a lightly floured board. Knead and roll out 1/4 inch thick. Put berries in baking dish and sprinkle with all but two Table-spoons sugar. Crisscross strips of dough 1/4 inch between strips. Sprinkle remainder of sugar over dough strips.

**Bake 450 degrees — 30 minutes.**

# CHOCOLATE PIE

**1-3/4 cups sugar**
**2 cups milk**
**3 Tablespoons butter**
**3 egg (yolks)**
**4 Tablespoons cocoa**
**6 Tablespoons flour**
**2-1/2 teaspoons vanilla**
**1 pie crust (9 inch)**

Mix sugar, milk, cocoa, egg yolks and flour. Cook over low heat until thick. Remove from heat. Add butter and vanilla. Mix well. Pour into pie crust and top with meringue.

### Meringue

Beat 3 egg whites until stiff peaks are formed. Add 2-1/2 Tablespoons sugar. Beat well. Spread over pie. Bake until meringue is golden brown.

**Bake 400 degrees.**

# COCONUT CREAM PIE

**3/4 cup sugar**
**5 Tablespoons flour**
**pinch of salt**
**1-3/4 cups milk**
**4 egg (yolks)**
**2 Tablespoons butter**
**1 teaspoon vanilla**
**2 cups coconut**
　　**(shredded)**

Mix sugar, flour and salt with 1/4 cup milk. Heat 1-1/2 cups milk and gradually stir into flour mixture. Cook on low heat until mixture begins to thicken. Add beaten egg yolks and cook 2-3 minutes. Remove from heat and stir in butter, vanilla and coconut. Pour into 9 inch pie shell.

*Top with meringue or whipped cream.*

# LEMON PIE

3/4 cup sugar
2 Tablespoons
    cornstarch
3/4 cup milk
3 egg (yolks)
3 Tablespoons lemon
    juice
1 teaspoon grated
    lemon peel
1 Tablespoon butter

Mix sugar and cornstarch. Add milk and egg yolks. Mix well. Cook over medium heat until mixture is thick, stirring constantly. Remove from heat and add lemon juice, lemon peel and butter. Pour into pie crust. Top with meringue if desired.

# PECAN PIE

1/2 cup brown sugar
1/2 cup sugar
4 Tablespoons flour
1 cup corn syrup
3 eggs
1 teaspoon vanilla
1 Tablespoon butter
    (softened)
2 cups pecans
    (chopped)

Sift dry ingredients. Add syrup, eggs, vanilla, butter and pecans. Mix well. Pour into pie shell.

**Bake 325 degrees — 45 minutes.**

# PIXIE PIE

1 cup butter
2 cups sugar
4 eggs (beaten)
2 teaspoons vinegar
2 teaspoons vanilla
1 cup coconut
    (shredded)
2 cups pineapple
    (crushed)
1 cup pecans (chopped)

Blend butter, sugar, eggs, vinegar and vanilla. Stir in coconut, pineapple and pecans. Pour into 9 inch pie shell.

**Bake 325 degrees — 50-55 minutes**

# SWEET POTATO PIE

**4 sweet potatoes (baked)**

**1/2 cup butter (softened)**

**2 cups sugar**

**4 eggs**

**1 teaspoon cinnamon**

**1/2 teaspoon salt**

**1 teaspoon nutmeg**

**1/4 teaspoon cloves**

**1-2/3 cups evaporated milk**

**15 marshmallows**

Peel potatoes and mash well. Blend in all ingredients except marshmallows. Pour into pie shells. Bake until firm. Remove from oven and top with marshmallows. Bake until marshmallows form light crust.

**Bake 350 degrees until firm.**
**Makes 2 pies**

# HOMEMADE VANILLA ICE CREAM

4 eggs (beaten)
2 cups sugar
2 Tablespoons flour
1 quart milk
2 pints (light cream)
1/2 pint whipping
    cream
1/2 teaspoon salt
1 Tablespoon vanilla

Mix all ingredients except vanilla in saucepan. Heat until little beads appear. Remove from heat and add vanilla. Mix well and pour into ice cream freezer.

**Makes 1 gallon.**

# BAKED CUSTARD

4 eggs
1 cup sugar
2 cups evaporated milk

Mix all ingredients. Beat until thoroughly mixed. Pour into pie shell, baking dish or custard dishes.

**Bake 300 degrees — 1-1/2 hours.**

*Sprinkle with nutmeg or choice of flavoring.*

# RICE PUDDING

4 eggs
2 cups milk
1/2 cup sugar
1 Tablespoon butter (melted)
1 teaspoon vanilla
1/4 teaspoon salt
2 cups rice (cooked)
1/2 cup raisins
1 teaspoon cinnamon
1/4 teaspoon nutmeg

Beat eggs and add milk, sugar, butter, vanilla and salt. Stir in rice and raisins. Pour into buttered baking dish. Sprinkle with cinnamon and nutmeg.

**Bake 325 degrees — 35 minutes.**

# CARAMEL POPCORN

2 sticks margarine
1/2 cup white syrup
2 cups brown sugar
1/4 teaspoon cream of
    tartar
1 teaspoon salt
1 teaspoon soda
6 quarts popped corn

Mix butter, syrup and sugar. Bring to boil for 6 minutes, stirring constantly. Remove from heat and add cream of tartar, salt and soda. Stir until foamy and pour over popped corn. Spread on cookie sheet after mixing.
**Bake 200 degrees — 1 hour.**

*Parched peanuts may be added*

# SUGAR COATED NUTS

5 cups pecans
pinch of salt
1/2 cup butter
1-1/2 cups sugar
5 egg whites (stiffly
    beaten)

Toast pecans until brown in 350 degree oven. Beat egg whites until stiff and fold in salt and sugar. Fold nuts into egg white mixture. Melt butter in shallow skillet. Pour pecan mixture into butter. Stir nuts occasionally while in oven.
**Bake 325 degrees — 20-30 minutes.**

# THAT OLD BLACK POT

That old black pot and depression days
Went together like the ocean and the waves.
You didn't go to the store back then,
And to waste a soup bone was considered a sin.
You grew what you ate and cooked what you got,
And it all came out of that old black pot.

There was cabbage, collards and turnip greens,
Okra, squash and string beans,
Black-eyed peas, onions and tomatoes,
Fat back, gravy and mashed potatoes.

The men rolled logs and plowed the fields
And prayed for rain that the crops might yield.
They picked the cotton and pulled the corn,
Built a shed for a calf newly born.
Oh, but the strength these men have 'got,'
And it all came out of that old black pot.

# Index

204

206

## STOKE GABRIEL ENTERPRISES, INC.
### P.O. BOX 12060 • ALEXANDRIA, LA 71315

Please send ___ copies **Old Black Pot Recipes** ...................................... $12.95 ea. $_____

Please send ___ copies **Big Mama's Back In The Kitchen** ...................... $14.95 ea. $_____

Plus postage and handling ......................................................................... $3.00 ea. $_____

Louisiana Residents add sales tax ........................................................... $ .52 ea. $_____

Enclosed is check ❏  money order ❏  ...................................... Total  $_____

Make checks payable to **Stoke Gabriel Enterprises. - No C.O.D.s**

### PLEASE PRINT OR TYPE

NAME _____

ADDRESS _____

CITY _____ STATE _____ ZIP _____

### ALLOW 2 WEEKS FOR DELIVERY

- - - - - - - - - - - - - - - - - - - - - - - - - - - - - - - - - - - - - - - - - - -

## STOKE GABRIEL ENTERPRISES, INC.
### P.O. BOX 12060 • ALEXANDRIA, LA 71315

Please send ___ copies **Old Black Pot Recipes** ...................................... $12.95 ea. $_____

Please send ___ copies **Big Mama's Back In The Kitchen** ...................... $14.95 ea. $_____

Plus postage and handling ......................................................................... $3.00 ea. $_____

Louisiana Residents add sales tax ........................................................... $ .52 ea. $_____

Enclosed is check ❏  money order ❏  ...................................... Total  $_____

Make checks payable to **Stoke Gabriel Enterprises. - No C.O.D.s**

### PLEASE PRINT OR TYPE

NAME _____

ADDRESS _____

CITY _____ STATE _____ ZIP _____

### ALLOW 2 WEEKS FOR DELIVERY

- - - - - - - - - - - - - - - - - - - - - - - - - - - - - - - - - - - - - - - - - - -

## STOKE GABRIEL ENTERPRISES, INC.
### P.O. BOX 12060 • ALEXANDRIA, LA 71315

Please send ___ copies **Old Black Pot Recipes** ...................................... $12.95 ea. $_____

Please send ___ copies **Big Mama's Back In The Kitchen** ...................... $14.95 ea. $_____

Plus postage and handling ......................................................................... $3.00 ea. $_____

Louisiana Residents add sales tax ........................................................... $ .52 ea. $_____

Enclosed is check ❏  money order ❏  ...................................... Total  $_____

Make checks payable to **Stoke Gabriel Enterprises. - No C.O.D.s**

### PLEASE PRINT OR TYPE

NAME _____

ADDRESS _____

CITY _____ STATE _____ ZIP _____

### ALLOW 2 WEEKS FOR DELIVERY